Taking the
Flower Show
Home

Published by Schiffer Publishing, Ltd.
4880 Lower Valley Road
Atglen, PA 19310
Phone: (610) 593-1777; Fax: (610) 593-2002
E-mail: Info@schifferbooks.com

For the largest selection of fine reference books on this and related subjects, please visit our website at
www.schifferbooks.com.
You may also write for a free catalog.

This book may be purchased from the publisher.
Please try your bookstore first.

We are always looking for people to write books on new and related subjects. If you have an idea for a book, please contact us at proposals@schifferbooks.com

Schiffer Books are available at special discounts for bulk purchases for sales promotions or premiums. Special editions, including personalized covers, corporate imprints, and excerpts can be created in large quantities for special needs. For more information contact the publisher.

In Europe, Schiffer books are distributed by
Bushwood Books
6 Marksbury Ave.
Kew Gardens
Surrey TW9 4JF England
Phone: 44 (0) 20 8392 8585; Fax: 44 (0) 20 8392 9876
E-mail: info@bushwoodbooks.co.uk
Website: www.bushwoodbooks.co.uk

4880 Lower Valley Road • Atglen, PA 19310

Taking the
Flower Show
Home Award-winning Designs
from Concept to Completion

Bill Schaffer AIFD, AAF, PFCI
Kristine Kratt AIFD, PFCI

CONTENTS

FOREWORD | Sam Lemheney

Senior Vice President for Shows and Events,
Pennsylvania Horticultural Society

The Philadelphia Flower Show started small. In 1829, two-dozen members of the two-year-old Pennsylvania Horticultural Society showed off their best fruits, vegetables, and favorite plants in a modest exhibition hall. But in that inaugural show and in subsequent years, this little circle of horticulturists introduced the American public to a world of new discoveries, including the dazzling poinsettia plant from Mexico, delicate peonies from China, sweet sugar cane from the West Indies, and the useful rubber tree from India.

Since those early years, the Flower Show has grown and blossomed. The 184-year-old show is now the largest indoor horticultural event in the world – covering 33 acres of exhibition floor and special event space in and around the Pennsylvania Convention Center – and it attracts more than a quarter-million visitors. The show still introduces new varieties of flowers and plants to the public, along with new products and techniques. But it has evolved into a multi-sensory experience of sights, scents, sound and tastes.

The show also has become a powerful economic engine, generating a $61 million impact on the Philadelphia region's business community.

The Flower Show is the major fundraiser for PHS as well, providing about $1 million annually for our year-round urban greening programs. Each ticket purchased supports our City Harvest program, which raises vegetables for residents who don't have access to fresh produce; our tree-planting campaign; educational projects that train gardeners of all ages; and efforts that help create community gardens, restore neighborhood parks, and reclaim vacant land. All of these programs are the 21st century missions of PHS, which has grown to more than 23,000 members across the U.S.

Of course, the Flower Show has another important purpose: to bring together the best floral and landscape designers, who create outstanding displays that entertain, educate, and inspire.

Which brings me to Schaffer Designs.

In the six years that Bill Schaffer and Kris Kratt have participated in the Flower Show, it has grown in amazing, innovative new directions, thanks in large part to their creativity, courage and energy. Bill and Kris have been a leading force in raising the level of design excellence throughout the Flower Show and, therefore, throughout the floral design industry.

I have encouraged our exhibitors to use the Flower Show as a canvas for new materials, new methods, and new ideas. Bill and Kris have embraced that opportunity and the possibilities inherent in the art of floral design.

Every exhibit by Schaffer Designs transports viewers to another world, from the dreamy depths of the ocean floor to a rollicking Hollywood movie set; from a transcendent Arctic haven to a red-hot volcanic eruption. All told through fantastic design and boundless, wild imagination.

Besides designing the Schaffer exhibits, which have become destination points for every visitor, Bill has brought added depth and enhanced the Flower Show in many other ways. He assisted in the development

of the Designer's Studio, an interactive venue where special guests present flower arranging demonstrations and where professionals and amateurs participate in live design competitions.

Bill's reputation in the floral industry has attracted applicants from around the U.S. and far beyond to the Flower Show. He has helped choose the best designers for the show and has been a valued consultant on finding young talent – a vital contribution that keeps the Philadelphia show exciting and ever changing.

Bill has also served as a fantastic ambassador for our show at other horticultural events around the globe. He has been invited to exhibit in the prestigious international competition in Singapore, and has addressed his colleagues and the public in other venues throughout the world. Bill is always eloquent and passionate about his work.

Schaffer Designs has been in the vanguard of floral designers because they always strive to create the unusual, unexpected, and dramatic.

It was only appropriate that Bill and Kris were married last year (2012) on the stage of the Flower Show with thousands of show guests as their witnesses. I'm so grateful that we were able to celebrate their happiness in the place and profession that has brought us all together.

Bill Schaffer and Kris Kratt have helped raise the level of great design not only in the Philadelphia show, but in the floral design industry around the world.

—Drew Becher, President of the Pennsylvania Horticultural Society

INTRODUCTION

Kris and I always wanted to "do" a floral design book. We've developed numerous ideas over the past few years, but we finally realized that some of the best design work that we have done together was at the Philadelphia Flower Show. We have been creating our own floral fantasy worlds at the Flower Show for six years and people always ask us to tell them how we do it. The answer for our first publishing collaboration was staring us in the face. If you are reading this, then you too wanted to learn a little bit more about what we do at the Flower Show. Now that you have purchased this book or borrowed it from someone who did or you are reading it at a friend's house … however you have this book in your hands, this is the story of Schaffer Designs™ at the Philadelphia Flower Show.

Before you read any further, we want you to know that exhibiting at the Flower Show is a true labor of love. The Philadelphia Flower Show is a great medium for Temporary Floral Art™. As designers, it allows us to push the boundaries of what we do and who we are. We find ourselves experimenting with techniques that we could never imagine using under normal design circumstances.

What a truly amazing opportunity it is. It should not be squandered on the same-old, been-there-done-that creations, but should be treated as a chance to push the limits of your abilities. To offer the attendee a peek into an ever-changing world of floral art is a responsibility that we take seriously. As we have come to learn, there are very few other arenas around the world that would allow us such freedom to be creative and to create.

Taking the Flower Show Home

Years ago, my mentors and friends encouraged me to participate at the Flower Show. Being the educators that Kris and I hope to be, we cannot think of a better opportunity to return that auspicious invitation than by welcoming others to share in our experience. The most rewarding feeling is when you take your idea, your baby, your months of planning and sketching and creating, and give that design to someone else to discover themselves in its completion. This book is the story of how we do it, but it is also a book about our forever-floral friends who come to share the experience with us.

In this book, Kris wrote the Section titled, *The Wedding* and created the book's layout; I wrote the balance of the text. Now – that is not to say that any part of the book wasn't worked on equally – we just could not figure out how to write it otherwise. Should we each write every other chapter, every other paragraph ... every other word? We found this method best to properly express our combined thoughts to you. What we have done is integrate the storytelling with quotes from our designers, storied text boxes, and hundreds of photographs. It is the telling of the behind-the-scenes trials-and-tribulations, ups-and-downs, and joy in the passion for what we do, for who we are. We hope you enjoy sharing it with us.

Chapter 1
FAIRIES

Pennsylvania Horticultural Society Flower Show Award
For *BEST IN SHOW* – Floral Design Category

Best Achievement Award
For Integration of Setting and Floral Design

EXHIBITOR'S INTENT

Explain the overall design concept of the exhibit:

Our inspiration was to capture a dark, Celtic forest, where within an enchanted circle of trees live the personalities of seven famed Fairies of Ireland.

Explain the horticultural concept of the exhibit:

We have chosen materials to contrast the dark, decaying forest with the vibrant hues of fresh flowers within the inner circle home of the Fairies.

What impact do you want the exhibit to have on the visitor?

The overall exhibit should give the visitor a newfound understanding of Ireland's Fairies.

The Flower Show had announced that the theme for the 2007 event would be "Legends of Ireland." As the announcement was made, the motif was decided. In 2005, I was a designer and the Co-Chair for the American Institute of Floral Designers' (AIFD) Exhibit. As a thank-you gift, the Chair presented me with a book called *Fairies*. The book was "filled with amazing illustrations and stories of a world charged with wild beauty." It seemed to make perfect sense. Schaffer Designs first endeavor at the Flower Show would come directly from inspiration derived from the Flower Show.

The research into the legends of the Fairies of Ireland showed not the sweet little, winged creatures of a child's Hollywood animation, but fierce clans representing seven major Irish Fairie families. "Fairies" was going to represent the dark side of the myth. Creating a contrast between the forbidden side of darkness and decay and its opposing side of light and beauty became the goal. To completely hide that wonder from the public's eye was to be the surprise.

I had begun developing ideas and sketching blueprints to be submitted to the Philadelphia Flower Show Board for approval. The sketches, let's just say, lacked maturity. How they were accepted is a mystery. It is probably the reason that Sam Lemheney introduced me to Chris Kanienberg, the owner of Wish Painting and Sculpture. He told me that he believed that we would be a good aesthetic fit. Chris is a master artist who is exceptional in all aspects of sculpture, painting, sketching, and prop construction. What Sam could not foresee is that Chris was to become the visual conscience for Schaffer Designs. Chris got it! He instantly started sketching design concepts. There was a definite learning curve between us. I quickly learned that whatever I asked him to do, he was going to find a way to make it happen.

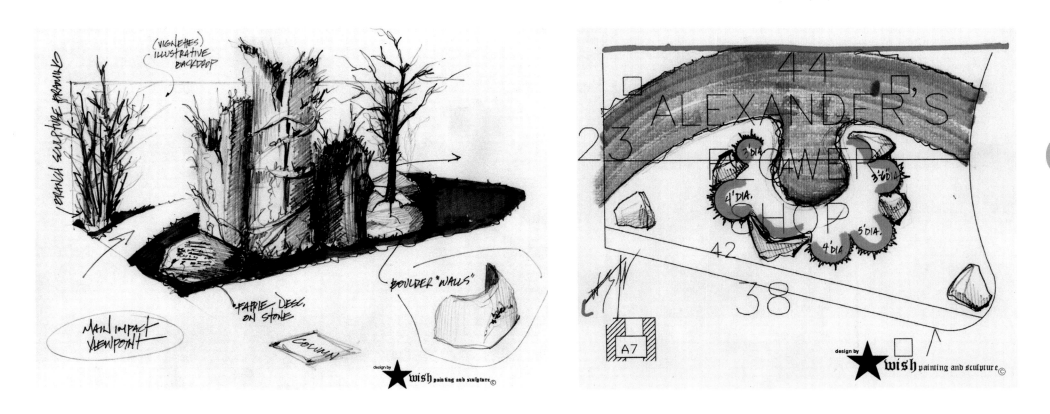

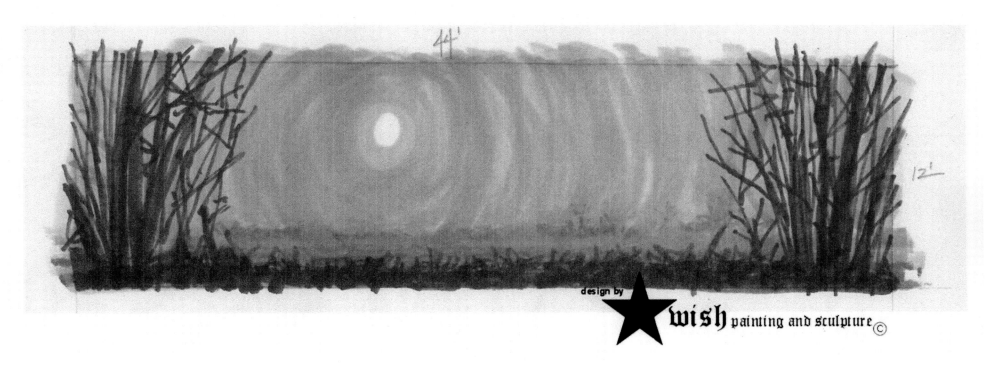

Taking the Flower Show Home

I had to open myself up to trusting his creativity. He needed to be educated on floral design and how it related to the props he was being asked to build.

I had seen many examples of his projects that helped to elevate my faith in him, but it wasn't until that first trip to his studio that I knew all was well. Chris had sketched out numerous overall and individual designs for me. We revised and revised again. We never lost sight of the dark glade of trees that I originally desired. We never lost sight of the emotions that we wanted to express and the emotions we hoped the attendees would feel. We decided to leave the exterior of the set a dark, barren, forsaken area. The designs were hidden behind the circular grove of massive tree trunks. Insulation foam, wood, nails, screws, and army surplus netting were just some of the materials used in the creation of our hidden glen. By the way, you may have noticed the use of the word "set." A set is what it had become – a Broadway stage of scenic floral design.

Work at the flower show has been among the hardest of things to describe when I am asked about what I do. Simply put, I don't do flowers, nor do I claim to know anything about them, beyond what looks good, and what doesn't. As a set designer, I focus each year on designing a "vehicle" for which to usher in the Schaffer Designs aesthetic. Florals are the passengers, the story …

—*Christian Kanienberg,*
Wish Painting & Sculpture

The behind-the-scenes reality is that, although we are judged on the opening day of the show, we must keep the exhibit Day One fresh throughout the entire nine days of the event. Consider a flower arrangement delivered to your home. How long does it remain fresh? How often do you have to replenish the water? How long does it last? Flowers for the show are delivered throughout the week leading up to the opening. We properly go through all the accepted floral industry standards of care and handling, but it is not enough. The flowers are put through a serious amount of stress during their life at the show. Diesel vapors, ethylene gas, emissions from cars and trucks, hot lights, and drastic in-house environmental temperature changes are only some of the trials that those delicate blossoms must endure. There is also the possibility of over a quarter of a million attendees' hands touching those stems close enough to be reached. All of this has to be managed throughout the show. Early morning and post-closing refreshing is a daily must! Just keeping fresh water in the exhibit is a serious commitment of time!

"Fairies" was Schaffer Designs' first undertaking into managing these challenges. Designs were created using floral foam, neoprene, steel armatures, wooden frames, glass vases, test tubes, and even a burial casket. The designs ranged from ground level up to fifteen feet high. The test was how to get all of this accomplished. This project was not going to be completed by my hands alone. My experiences at the Philadelphia Flower Show educated me in the realization that I needed a talented, strong, trustworthy group of people to assist me. Five months before the first flower entered the Pennsylvania Convention Center, I began reaching out to many designers I had met over the years. Phone calls and e-mails were in abundance. I spoke with dozens

of designers. I only had six Principle Designer spots available. I asked too many people. So many talented people wanted to participate. It became a "first come, first serve" decision. In the end, a team of seven principle designers (including myself) was assembled. I couldn't have been happier with the friends who were coming from around the United States and from other countries. The set designs were finalized, materials for construction were being acquired and props were being built.

"Fairies" was my first opportunity to contribute to the creativity that is Schaffer Designs … Although I was just in charge of the 'leaf litter' and the outer flora of the display, I was participating: I was hooked.

—*David Hamilton*

There are a number of elements involved in floral design on this scale. The first is selecting the designers. The second is the design itself. I wanted the individual designers to be able to create their own piece. Each design was to reflect the ideas and talents of the individual so that the characteristics of the different Fairie groups were obvious. The third element needed to create this type of design is control of product and color. The view of the Fairies was a semi-circle of florals. It was the perfect visual for a representation of the color wheel. With that in mind, each designer was assigned a specific space, given the physical parameters and each was given an analogous color grouping to work with. The final element for the successful composition was the history of each clan. Months were spent researching the characteristics of the individual Irish Fairie families and each designer was given multiple reference chapters and renderings in sketches and paintings of their respective Fairie. All were then asked to do their homework and design their interpretations. A whole new series of phone calls and e-mails began that lasted almost three months as each designer did their homework, made their flower and supply request lists, and called to discuss their plans and share ideas.

Such an extraordinary experience "Fairies" was for me to see the big scale of floral exhibits for the first time.
—Donald Yim

The designers had their jobs and were going to be too busy to help shovel a few tons of dirt into layered mounds or to precisely place dozens of bags of fallen and dried leaves, twigs, and branches. We had a thousand pounds of colored glass, Belgian block borders, and so many other set details to place that it was going to take a small army to accomplish it all. A small army is exactly what volunteered to assist the designers and complete these tasks and many others. Unboxing and processing all of the flowers, trudging hundreds of gallons of water for flower buckets, assisting the designers in their needs, and cleaning up every night so that the next day started pristine. My family and friends, friends of friends, and so many in and out of the floral industry responded to my requests for help. It was amazing! Laughter filled the set for the whole week, but it did not start out that way.

The move-in day at the Convention Center was a full week before the Show was scheduled to open. Everything was organized. Every plan was in place and

just waiting for its time. Vehicles met at the bottom of the ramp at the Pennsylvania Convention Center filled with props and supplies to begin their inward march. As we drove into that grand hall, the moment that had been planned and prepped for one full year was about to come. We were among the very first groups to enter and unload. The relief, excitement, wonderment, and joy quickly faded to fear and paranoia as all of the trucks, vans, and people pulled away and I was left standing in this nearly empty, cavernous building. The Flower Show is 33 acres of beauty. This was cold. A vast, barren landscape of concrete, 40-foot windowless walls, ceilings filled with harsh lights and intermittent columns the size of cement-poured, forsaken redwoods. I was standing alone with our entire set in its 1200 square foot space. It seemed so small. It was too late to turn back now.

A fantastical telling would be to say that all went smoothly. Our 44' long, 12' high canvas painting of a moonlit backdrop was seriously ripped in several spots as a result of its hanging; flowers arrived late with the wrong color and the wrong varieties; designers had trains and planes whose schedules were ever-changing; a non-stop litany of paperwork from the Show's offices needed attending to; multiple union workers converged on the set at the same time; numerous last-minute trips were made to the hardware store; jobs needed to be found for the ever-increasing cast of volunteers; and there were 16 hour days of waiting, waiting and more waiting. Finally, it was almost 2 a.m. on the final day before the lighting was completed and all was ready to go. Then, while the lights were being spotted, one of the cranes lifting the lighting technicians began leaking. From 30 feet in the air it began raining motor oil onto one of our custom-printed signs and all over the floor. Did I happen to mention that I was also one of the designers?

It was a joy to experience so many coming together with just one goal in mind. It would have been better if I hadn't almost overwhelmed myself with responsibilities. By the time I started advance preparation for my design, it was a mere month before the show was to open. "The show must go on" and that is exactly what was going to happen whether I was ready or not. I knew I needed help. I reached out to a friend I had met while we were both on the Membership Committee of American Institute of Floral Designers.

Kristine Kratt was living just outside of Dallas, Texas, in a small suburban city called Flower Mound (how appropriate). She immediately jumped at the opportunity to assist. Well, in my mind she jumped at the opportunity – in actuality, I think she felt sorry for me in my desperation. Though the final product had my name on it, it could just as easily have been emblazoned with both of our names. Kris took all of my ideas, sketches, colors, and flower lists and converted them into a layered series of coherent design sketches. My chosen Fairie was the Leprechaun. In Irish Folklore, the Leprechaun was a cobbler. Kris took it upon herself to create dozens of floral shoes. She reached out to her family and friends and collected boots, heels, sneakers, men's dress shoes and more to create a whole range of Floral Leprechaun shoes out of dried floral and other natural materials for the exhibit.

Kris also aided in editing all of the poems and other text that I was writing for the displays. One of the most important is the Exhibitor Intent Form. It is from this document that the judges score your exhibit, based on the successful completion of your objectives. Kris also introduced me to her brother, Bill Kratt, who designed my new company logo and also did the graphic designs for the entire exhibit. What a relief! Everything was finally under control.

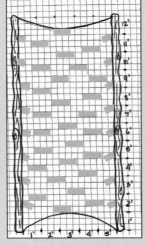

Emerging from the misty forest glade, the moon's glow leads you to the edge of the wood. No, not the moon, but an enticing radiance that dances behind a ring of trees and rock. Turn away – you should – but beyond is a world of dark enchantments, of captivating beauty, joy, and inspiration, laughter and love. In the ring are the Fairies and a magical door to their realm. Take heed, it is a world to enter with extreme caution, for of all things that Fairies resent most it is curious humans blundering about their private domains like so many ill-mannered tourists. So go softly – where the rewards are enchanting and the dangers are real.

Taking the Flower Show Home

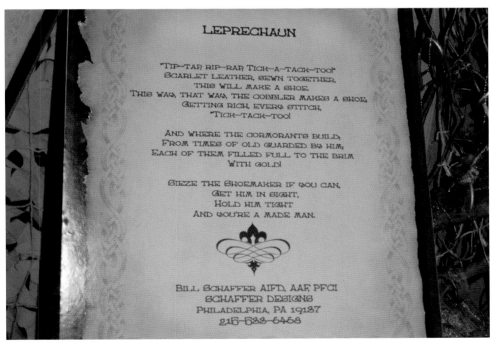

LEPRECHAUN

"Tip-tap rip-rap Tick-a-tack-too!"
Scarlet leather, sewn together,
This will make a shoe.
This way, that way, the cobbler makes a shoe,
Getting rich, every stitch,
Tick-tack-too!

And where the cormorants build,
From times of old guarded by him,
Each of them filled full to the brim
With gold!

Sieze the shoemaker if you can,
Get him in sight,
Hold him tight
And you're a made man.

❧

Bill Schaffer AIFD, AAF, PFCI
Schaffer Designs
Philadelphia, PA 19187
215-633-6468

Taking the Flower Show Home

I walked into the Philadelphia Flower Show for the very first time — from the bitter, winter cold outside into the colors, textures, and overwhelming fragrance of floral electricity. Until I entered the doors and saw it in person, I could not have imagined the sheer size of it. It made me feel like a small creature in an immense garden. I wanted to explore every twist and turn of its pathways. The excitement and anticipation of experiencing each new area let me know that this show was somewhere truly special to be.

—Kristine Kratt

Taking the Flower Show Home

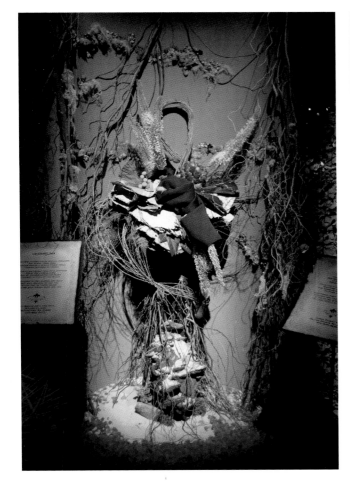

Looking back now, I understand that all of the previously mentioned glitches are normal. I could just as easily have stated that the move-in was smooth, the arrival of the flowers and supplies went as scheduled, and the designers arrived on time. What actually happened was that all week I was filled with dread of something that I could not handle. It never happened. It all came together with professionalism and professional courtesies. Designers, family, friends, and other volunteers all connected as a real team. Complete advance preparation and organization mixed with dedicated teamwork is the key to a successful display at the Philadelphia Flower Show. We were ready. It was show time!

The Members Only Day began on Saturday, and the judging started at 7 in the morning the same day. By the time I awoke that morning and got to the Convention Center, it was just before the doors opened to begin Members Only Day. Waiting nervously for any decision is one of the most stressful periods of time I have ever experienced. Almost three hours elapsed – the wait was stretching into an eternity. Then, without any pomp and circumstance, a woman approached the exhibit with a large silver cup in her hands, reached into the exhibit and placed it on the ground as another woman was hanging a sign that read:

The Pennsylvania Horticulture Society's
Flower Show Award
Presented to a Major Exhibitor as the
BEST IN SHOW
Floral Design

I almost dropped to the ground. Tears were in my eyes. Hundreds of people I didn't know began cheering aloud! It was an amazing sensation! All I wanted to do

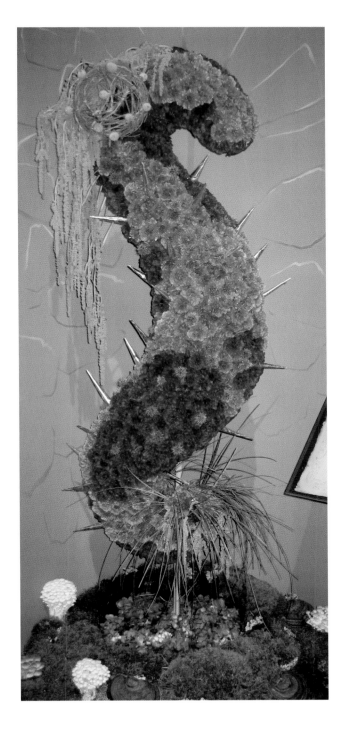

was share it with all of the team that had helped make this a success. I spent the next couple of hours on the phone contacting everyone involved. The immediate accolades were short-lived as I realized I had to be back that night for the first cleanup and refresh of the long nine days of the show.

My favorite memory of that first year had nothing to do with the actual design and construction of the exhibit. My fascination came from the throngs of people trying to see what was behind the grove of trees. They saw shards of light, bits of color, and their curiosity took over. All that planning was actually working. The exhibit was designed for the viewers to walk in one side and out the other. Numerous directional signs were in place to state that fact. It did not matter. As one group of people merged with the groups entering from the opposite side, it became an overwhelming sea of people with no easy exit. For the first time in the history of the flower show, the powers-that-be decided to put rows and rows of stanchions outside the exhibit, directing the mass of people into and out of the floral design area in a controlled way. Like at a Disney World ride, they waited to enter, most for almost 15-20 minutes. There were 3-4 hours every day when the wait would be from 45 minutes to a full one-hour. The outside of the exhibit, with its dark recesses and hidden floral gems, kept their senses occupied as they got closer and closer. As the attendees neared the entrance and actually entered, the display was filled with the history of the Fairies in descriptions of the designs and original poems. The contrast of the dark, dismal exterior was wildly changed with the brightly lit and colorful circle of flowers on the inside. The crowds seemed to really enjoy it. I found myself giving private tour after tour. By Day Five, I could barely talk from a sore throat, but didn't let it stop me! I was having the floral time of my life!

Taking the Flower Show Home

Taking the Flower Show Home

INTERPRETATION

As shown here, we have created two individual designs; one hidden and the other visible to show both sides of this style arrangement. This translation of the original Flower Show Exhibit is to be viewed from both sides. As the viewer moves around the piece, they are surprised with the hidden Fairie garden found on the opposite side. By completing the composition from each aspect, the additional interest to the textural wooded side is heightened with the anticipation of what is to come.

MATERIALS

15" black designer dish
6" black designer dish
Birch strips
Butterflies
Chicken wire
OASIS® standard foam bricks (2)
OASIS® pan glue
3'-4' moss-coated birch branches
Moss mat – preserved/green
Moss, fresh sheet
Moss, reindeer – spring green
Moss, Spanish
Paint brush, small
Sticks, wooden

FLOWERS

Boronia heterophylla, hot pink
Celosia plumosa
Gerbera daisy, hot pink 'Whisper'
Lathyrus odoratus, dark pink (sweet pea)
Liatris spicata
Rosa, 'Purple Haze'

CONSTRUCTION

To create the "hidden Fairie tree," use hot glue to adhere two dry bricks of floral foam to the container. After allowing the glue to cool, fully soak the container with the glued floral foam in water.

Measure the size of the outer diameter of the container where you will be placing the tree. When measuring, keep in mind that your final design should feel as though it is hidden. Cut moss mat sheet and chicken wire to size; in a 15" diameter tray/dish this would be approximately 30". Using a small paint brush, paint on the hot glue to adhere the moss mat, chicken wire and, multiple strips of bark to form both the inner and outer "tree" (uneven strips of bark add interest to the final design).

Shape the tree form to fit around the floral foam; use wooden sticks to skewer the base of the "tree" into the wet floral foam. Cover all visible mechanics with reindeer moss. The reindeer moss can also be added as a decorative accent on the tree.

Insert the materials with the strongest parallel lines (liatris and moss coated birch branch) into the floral foam. Design each of the floral types into groups, giving each floral product a clear-cut color blocking. Use Spanish moss to cover the remainder of the floral foam (first, to hide the balance of the mechanics, and second, to add a complimenting color with the bark and texture for additional interest).

Design with the balance of the flowers. In this study, the flowers are tucked in low, toward the front of the design and gain elevation as they are inserted – moving back through the composition. This adds visual depth and rhythm to the completed design.

Chapter 2

JAZZED

Flower Show Award of SAF – Society of American
Florists Flower Show Award for Artistic Presentation of
Flowers and Plants for Public

Best Achievement Award for Imaginative Floral Design

Special Achievement Award of the Garden Club of Pennsylvania
Awarded to Exhibits of Unusual Excellence
in the Category of Creativity (over 1,000 SF)

EXHIBITOR'S INTENT

Explain the overall design concept of the exhibit:
Our Inspiration was to capture an ageless Jazz Club, where the patron's
emotions are enhanced by the music and reflected in color.
Explain the horticultural concept of the exhibit:
We have chosen materials to accentuate the blending of music and the
vibrant hues of flowers within and surrounding the inhabitants of the Jazz
Club.
What impact do you want the exhibit to have on the visitor?
The exhibit should give a glimpse into a world where emotions come to life
as everyone is transformed into reflections of their feelings through flowers.

In creating an installation on the scale of the
Philadelphia Flower Show exhibits, creative teams go
through various methods to find their ideas. The Flower
Show gives you the initial inspiration by announcing its
theme. The theme for 2008 was "*Jazz It Up*" and was
to feature the sights, sounds, and fragrances of New
Orleans. This year was a relatively easy year to reach
inside and find the inner muse. Both Kris and I had
visited New Orleans separately and we both had fallen
in love with its style and especially its flowers. A life long
passion for music led to the decision to feature rhythm
as the principal focus of our designs.

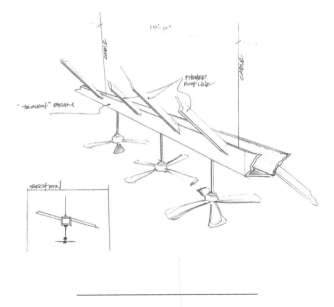

*Hot can be cool, and cool can be hot,
and each can be both. But hot or cool,
man, jazz is jazz.*
—*Louis (Satchmo) Armstrong,
jazz trumpeter and singer*

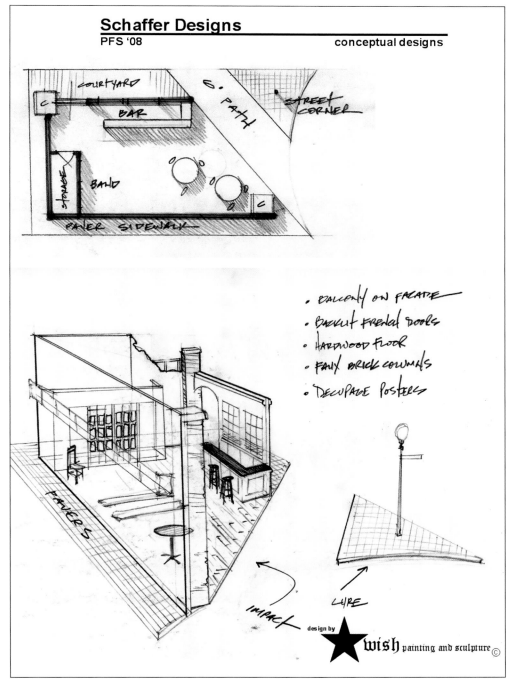

Schaffer Designs
PFS '08   conceptual designs

COURTYARD
6' PATH
STREET CORNER
BAR
BAND
STORAGE
PAVER SIDEWALK

- BALCONY ON FACADE
- BACKLIT FRENCH DOORS
- HARDWOOD FLOOR
- FAUX BRICK COLUMNS
- DECUPAGE POSTERS

PAVERS

IMPACT

LYRE

design by ★ wish painting and sculpture ©

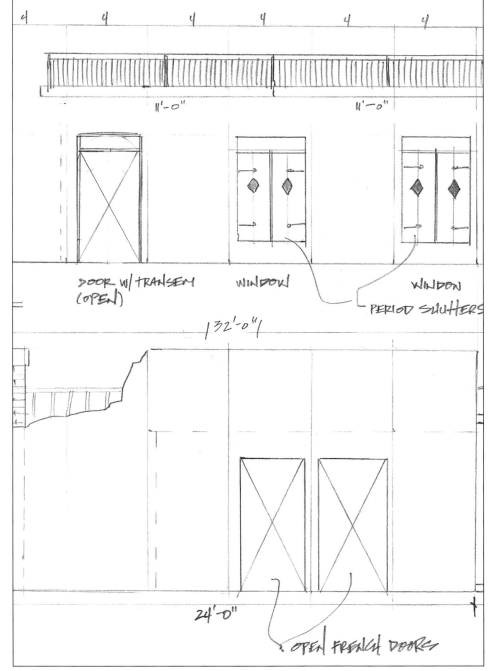

11'-0"   11'-0"

DOOR W/ TRANSEM   WINDOW   WINDOW
(OPEN)
                         PERIOD SHUTTERS

132'-0"

24'-0"   OPEN FRENCH DOORS

The first full-time collaboration of Kris and Bill had begun. Sometimes when an idea grows, it is accompanied by its own story. We began discussing our ideas in June 2007 and after a month realized that bullet points on a piece of paper were not going to do it. So, we wrote the story's scene.

Jazz, Rue'Bourbon, 1925 ... in the heart of NOLA. From outside you are drawn to the sounds of the rhythm. A cool bass accompanies your walk as you glide to the black and whites. As you approach, the worn-shingled, pocked-plaster exterior of the nightclub does little to convey the rich sounds emanating from within. The familiar smell of an old bar, the Gulf Stream sweat, and perfume of the customers permeates your senses as you enter. The only relief comes from over-sized, rusted ceiling fans. You are immediately drawn to the music ... the band sits on their throne...a small, poorly lit stage with tattered old velvet curtains, but the music...cool ...and the couple dancing...hot. You walk into the room; at the back is Joe, pouring drinks and dispensing his advice to those draining their souls. Looking for a table, you see a couple on their first date, an inebriated wretch passed-out next to his drink, some workers unwinding from their week, and more. A table near the stage is where you are seated ... you and your love ... you reach across the table, hands intertwined as you gaze into each other's eyes.

Emotions come to life as topiary frames of the nightclub's clientele and employees are transformed into reflections of their feelings through the world of flowers. As the piano player's fingers shoot white into the keys, bursting forth from the ivories are the colors of the night, while the cool, bluesy sounds of the bass player are reflected in the blue florals emanating from his soul through the bass. The bartender is a reflection of darkness as he is drained of color by the pull of the worries of the world. Our drunken soul is beaten black and blue from life ...the group of workers with similar thoughts whose emotions are analogous. Our dancing friends; a hierarchy of awareness through orange and chartreuse. Finally, our couple in love, as rich reds start in their hearts, playing with the tints and hues as their hands meet back into the height of the red in their hearts.

We had our story. Many of the individual elements would change, but the strong sense of emotions through flowers continued to grow. We needed a better setting than just an everyday bar or club. We wanted it to embody the feel and sounds of New Orleans. Located in the French Quarter, just three blocks from the Mississippi River is the Preservation Hall and its ever-famous Preservation Hall Jazz Band. We couldn't think of a better way to make "Jazzed" come to life than by putting it on that stage. Of course, that stage had to be built and Wish Painting & Sculpture was invited back for round two of our Flower Show connection.

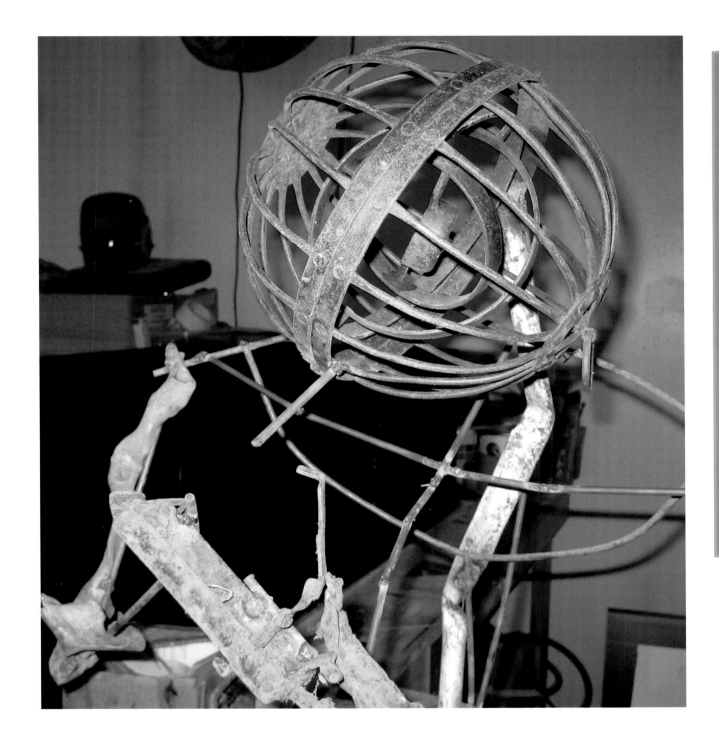

Jazzed was my first full partnership with Bill on an exhibit for the Philadelphia Flower Show. The planning was such an amazing collaboration of ideas. We realized just how well our concepts combined together to create an even better big picture than either of us could have painted alone.

When the day came to load it all into the convention center, it was such a blend of excitement, combined with a bit of intimidation and a dash of being totally overwhelming. The show floor was a rumble of chaotic activity … big trucks, forklifts, and massive construction covered every part of it. It was hard to believe that, in just a few days, this would all be perfect and ready for the public to walk through.

The set came alive and our design plans began to emerge from all the helping hands around us. It was just as we had imagined it … a product of our passion for design and our passion for each other.

—Kristine Kratt

Taking the Flower Show Home

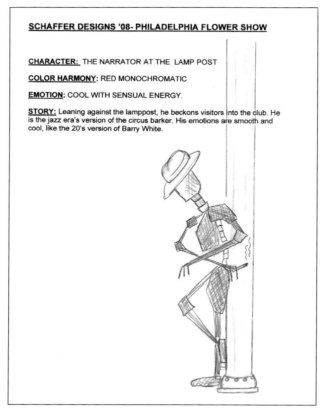

SCHAFFER DESIGNS '08- PHILADELPHIA FLOWER SHOW

CHARACTER: THE NARRATOR AT THE LAMP POST

COLOR HARMONY: RED MONOCHROMATIC

EMOTION: COOL WITH SENSUAL ENERGY.

STORY: Leaning against the lamppost, he beckons visitors into the club. He is the jazz era's version of the circus barker. His emotions are smooth and cool, like the 20's version of Barry White.

I will never take for granted the unique opportunities that allow me the chance to fabricate for the show each year. I had to pinch myself when I was having such fun welding together steel and found objects to make figural armatures for "Jazzed" back in early 2008. I knew then that I had a coveted position as an artist, making a living ... by making art. It was totally liberating.

—Christian Kanienberg, Wish Painting & Sculpture

Photographs of the exterior and the interior of Preservation Hall were gathered. The previous year's attendees' lines had to give way to a more open feel, yet still ask the audience to intimately participate with the florals. As with "Fairies," we wanted this set to be excruciatingly detailed. We wanted to project a dark, neglected, seedy feel to the exterior and interior walls of the club. The goal was to make the set be intimately involved in the experience of the overall exhibit, but able to stand alone as a very cool art installation.

We found the mediums of sculpture, painting, old jazz posters—basically anything that an Internet search engine could inspire. We were out shopping in a national chain store, not thinking about the Flower Show, when we literally turned into an aisle and found a hand-sized, wired sculpture of a jazz band. We were inspired to turn this piece into life-sized forms. Kanienberg had the great idea of creating these sculptures out of found, rusted bits and pieces of metal objects all welded together. Kris took that concept and sketched drawings of what our final pieces were to look like.

At the same time we were developing the final look of the set and its characters, we were also targeting the individual emotions that would be displayed by each of the characters or groups of figures. We had previously created the story with the basic emotions for each group and used that as the springboard for our final direction. We wanted our designers to have an individual background for each of the "people" and gifted them with their own story. We sifted through hundreds of quotes by famous jazz musicians and singers to instill each with their own personality.

SCHAFFER DESIGNS '08- PHILADELPHIA FLOWER SHOW

CHARACTER: THE DRUNK AT THE BAR

COLOR HARMONY: ANALOGOUS- BLUE, BLUE VIOLET, VIOLET

EMOTION: DEPRESSED

STORY: Saddened by life, the music only pushes the drunk further into a deep, melancholy state. His emotions seep down his body.

As a young designer, I had never been involved in anything like this production. I'd been to the show in years past, but never considered what it took to put it together. I fell in love with the set itself, the lazy fans spinning over-head and the "people" composed of parts and flowers. In my eyes it was genius ... I learned how to manipulate callas, string roses and make mechanics look like they belong ... my favorite had to be the couple, holding hands across the table ... but then again, I'm a sucker for flowers and for love!"
—Renee Tucci

Taking the Flower Show Home

In 2007, "Fairies" was an education for us in so many ways, including the what-to-do and what-not-to-do experiences. This time, along with the character history, each of the designers also received a letter containing the following instructions:

CONTAINERS – no visible containers are to be used unless they are part of the mechanics – an example would be water tubes – vases used as a water source that becomes part of the design. Spray bars or any products that do not have a long-term water source are not to be used. Containers will be provided in a rust color to match the sculptures if you can provide your container needs before this week's end. Containers can be tied to the sculpture with matching cable ties; containers can be placed on the floor as long as they are hidden.

FLORALS – flowers to be used should be of high quality and long lasting abilities … flowers need to be changed only once during the flower show. Flowers must last from Thursday, Feb. 28 through Wednesday, March 5 before full changeover is necessary … keep in mind a good water source. All floral procurement orders should be placed by Friday, Feb. 22, 2008. Any questions on florals or containers please feel free to call me.

DESIGN – though I know that many of you already have your design concept in mind – feel free to consider that the body of the sculpture is not the limitations of your design … go up, go down, inward – outward – use armatures, containers, multiple water sources … be open to create the design with numerous areas as a focal center considering that multiple designs may be created out of one sculpture as long as the overall concept is kept in place or a single continuous design, etc.

SETUP – flowers are scheduled to arrive Wednesday, February 27, 2008 and will be conditioned and ready for design work on Thursday. We can start by 8am on Thursday and go until 6pm and from 8am – 8pm on Friday (or as late as necessary) – lighting is scheduled for 9pm-10pm on Friday night.

Taking the Flower Show Home

Taking the Flower Show Home

Taking the Flower Show Home

Setting up an exhibit at the Flower Show is always intense. "Jazzed" was not going to be any different. As the first of three 24-foot box trucks loaded with the set arrived at the Flower Show, my son, Andrew, and I patiently waited to be a part of the move-in crew. Dozens of 8-foot and 12-foot faux wall panels were unloaded, an actual 12-foot wooden bar, a completely faux-finished dance floor, an 8-foot "brick" chimney stack, gas lights, ladders, buckets of touch-up paint, tool chests, instruments, table, chairs, stools, doors, window frames, and, of course, the stars of the show – the musicians, dancers, guests, bartender, barmaid, and other invited guest sculptures. We had only two days to assemble our representation of the Preservation Hall, which included suspending a 14-foot long structure with three ceiling fans, before the flowers were to be delivered and the floral design team was on site.

The three-sided building of our Preservation Hall had a dedicated crew from our set designer, including a small team of painters who were giving our walls a faux and découpage finish. Multiple crews from the different laborer's unions were involved in set construction, electrical wiring for the fans, lighting, even a crew for laying in the stone pathways and cutting stone for the street corner. Now that may seem like a lot of people – and it is! For each union you have to go to their respective offices and apply for a work order.

You hope for an early start time! We were lucky! We were one of the first to have a crew assigned to us. During the first two days of setup and construction we had as many as thirty workers putting the exhibit together at any one time. Of course, that were continuously interrupted by multiple contracted breaks, lunches, and deciphering which group had responsibility for which part of a job. If the electric line ran up a wall, did that fall under the jurisdiction of the electrical union or the carpenter's union? That question took more than 24 hours to answer and

another 24 hours to get a crew assigned to the job. Suffice it to say that, by the time the designers arrived, they still had two more days of working around the laborers. Up to fifty people occupied the space. The 1,200 square foot exhibit became a tight squeeze.

As Schaffer Designs Year Two entered full on site production, we had grown. In 2007, we had seven Principle Designers and ten other designers and volunteers on site. In 2008, we went from a project to a production, with eight Principle Designers and a cast of another dozen on the design team. The commotion and clutter around us, which we had no control over, never hindered our progress. The installation was filled with numerous complications but, just like the music leading our way, we improvised.

It's the group sound that's important, even when you're playing a solo. You not only have to know your own instrument, you must know the others and how to back them up at all times. That's jazz.
—*Oscar Peterson, jazz pianist*

We get to do such wonderful things in life. Creating public enjoyment with our talent. Working with family and friends. Educating others. Giving opportunities where they didn't exist before. Life is amazing! In the first chapter, the old cliché of "the show must go on" was mentioned. This year it could not have been truer. As the hundreds of thousands of people moved through the hall, they were oblivious to the fact that there were two people who would not get to share in any more of life's joys. During the Show, Kris's mother and my sweet, ten-year-old nephew passed. We continued to improvise.

Taking the Flower Show Home

INTERPRETATION

When analyzing the designs for The Flower Show exhibit "Jazzed," you see that they are entirely made up of welded steel, sculpted characters representing inhabitants of a New Orleans jazz club. Here, we use the commonly found, everyday form of a tomato cage to create the feel of the exhibit. Instead of recreating the appearance of a person, this design focuses on the rhythmic movement of the music. As the flowers and other materials spiral upwards from a strong base, they drift off into the ether as the beat continues. As with a "live" musical performance, this design is for the moment. With the structure completed, you can recreate and/or re-envision this piece over-and-over again.

MATERIALS

6" glass water tubes
Cable-ties, bright green
OASIS® Apple Green flat cane
OASIS® floral adhesive, tube
Plastic bowl
Quick-set cement, 10 pounds
Stapler and staples
Tomato cage, powder-coated yellow

FLOWERS

Craspedia globosa
Leucospermum, pincushion protea, yellow
Mokara, 'Nora' brown
Pandanus (variegated hala)
Zantedeschia, 'Treasure' (mini calla)

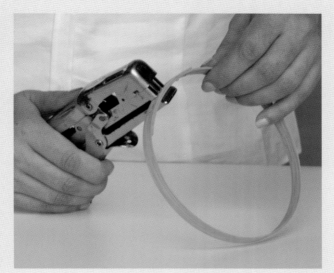

CONSTRUCTION

The assembly of this design should be started at least 1-2 hours before flower insertions are to be made. Clean and dry a basic round plastic bowl (at least 12" in diameter). Mix Quick-Set cement according to directions. On a level surface, pour the cement mixture into the plastic bowl. Wait 3-5 minutes; then insert the tomato cage. Allow the cement to harden (during the drying process the mixture becomes quite hot and should not be moved).

While the cement mixture is drying, begin cutting 40 strips of the flat cane into 2 lengths, one about 18" and the other about 12". To create each circle; overlap each end by 1", then staple the ends together. The entire length of circles can be created on the design table by stapling each circle together, one-by-one.

After the cement has dried and hardened, carefully remove the plastic bowl. Place the length of the circled flat cane onto the tomato cage using cable ties to secure it in place. Add additional circles of flat cane, if desired, to complete the spiraled motion.

To add additional lines to this arrangement, use the pandanus to strengthen the visual movement. Using a knife, cut a straight edge to the base of the foliage. Split the foliage about 1-½". Place the split base of the foliage on of the legs of the tomato cage and bring the piece across the cage. Bend the pandanus over the first ring of the tomato cage and bring the remainder back across the length of the ring. Take the remaining top-end of the foliage and loop around the ring; overlap and staple to secure. Repeat this process again on the next level up.

Using cable-ties, connect the glass water tubes to the structure. Use 2 cable-ties for each; one at the top and another at the base. This will keep the lines of the water tubes vertical and clean. Keep the placement of the water tubes random. This will allow for greater artistry for the floral designing process. Use the natural movement of the flowers to create the rhythm of the design. Mokara florets are used to reflect the concept of music notes floating through the air. Dab the back of the floret and the location where it is to be placed with floral adhesive; wait a minute to allow a strong tack to form and then bond into position.

Chapter 3
ARRIVEDERCI ATLANTIS

Best Achievement Award
for Best Dramatic Use of Color

EXHIBITOR'S INTENT

Explain the overall design concept of the exhibit:
To create a finely crafted mix of florals and setting to tell a story that allows the visitor to experience a fantasy world.
Explain the horticultural concept of the exhibit:
Natural materials have been selected, creating an underwater environment. Carnations, tropical, curly willow or palm fibers, nature doesn't have favorites when showing off it's beauty.
What impact do you want the exhibit to have on the visitor?
To evoke that childlike wonderment for the legend of Atlantis and an appreciation for the floral designs that brought it to life.

A long time ago, the great scholar, Plato, wrote of an island off of the coast of Italy. This island was called Atlantis. Atlantis was the mortal home of the worshipers of Neptune, the Roman god of the sea. For generations, Atlanteans lived simple, virtuous lives. As millennia passed, Atlantis became the legendary island of great and marvelous power, inhabited by scholars who isolated themselves in the pursuit of philosophy. Atlantis had scientists with inventions beyond our imagination. It was the perfect civilization, but it slowly began to change. Greed and power began to corrupt its people. By 9600 B.C., Atlantis became a naval power that conquered many lands.

As their god, when Neptune looked upon them he saw the immorality of the Atlanteans and was angered. He ordered his son Triton, the "Messenger of the Sea," to raise his horn and call upon all the mermen and mermaids of the world to announce the end of

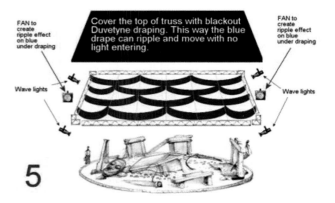

5

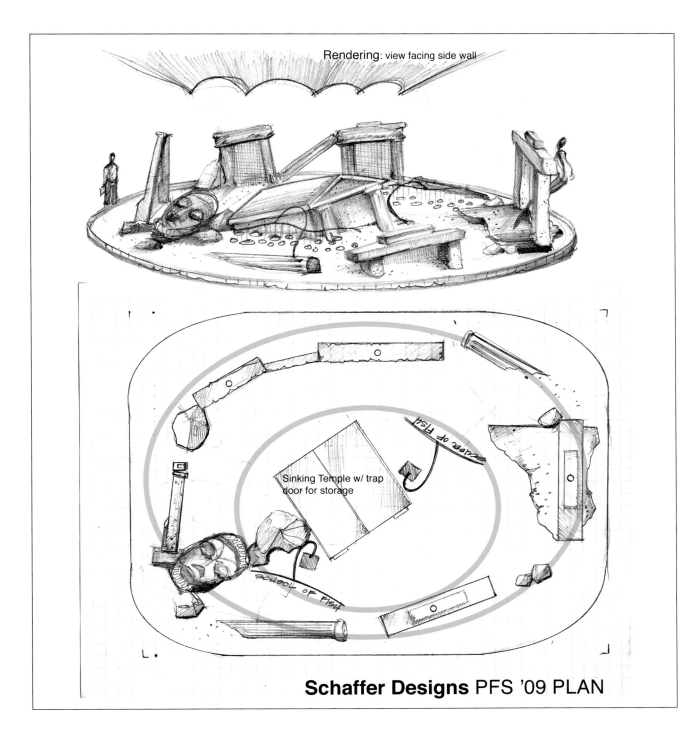

Rendering: view facing side wall

Sinking Temple w/ trap door for storage

Schaffer Designs PFS '09 PLAN

Atlantis. When Neptune raised his Trident against Atlantis and struck the ground with it, earthquakes rumbled, volcanoes were ignited, and the sea itself came to life. Plato wrote, "… there occurred portentous earthquakes and floods, and one grievous day and night befell them, when the whole body of your warriors was swallowed up by the earth, and the island of Atlantis in like manner was swallowed up by the sea and vanished; wherefore also the ocean at that spot has now become impassable and unsearchable …"

This became our inspiration for the 2009 Philadelphia Flower Show with the theme "Bella Italia." The beautiful gardens, terraces and landscapes of Italy were on everyone's list. The ancient architecture of the Coliseum, the Pantheon, St. Peter's, and all of the most well known historical locations were expected. A darker undercurrent rang through our previous themes and we naturally decided to follow that direction in 2009. To expect the unexpected was becoming the *modus operandi* of Schaffer Designs. Being a lifelong fan of the world's mythologies, the Roman gods have always been a fascination.

In a number of texts, we discovered early writings that connected Neptune to Atlantis and Atlantis to an island off of the coast of Italy. We had it! We may have been pushing the limits of historical fact, but this is about creating a fantasy and that illusion is what we were going to give the visitors.

We had success with the characters created in "Jazzed," but felt that we hadn't taken them far enough. In "Jazzed," the flowers were an extension of the sculptures; here we wanted to finish what we started by incorporating the floral design into the engineering of the sculpture. Merpeople were to be the inspiration for our designs. Research led us to discover that cultures all over the planet developed similar mythologies about

Taking the Flower Show Home

Taking the Flower Show Home

these half-human, half-fishlike beings. Once we had our concepts locked in, it was time to call our set designer and get to work.

Sketches, rewrites of the script, and more sketches led us to believe that we needed more input into this than just the three of us. This was the first time that our formula for brainstorming through a design "think tank" emerged. We called several meetings with other floral and set designers, graphic specialists, and lighting engineers. To give the feeling of the set being underwater, we developed an overhead rigging system of almost 1,000 yards of deep blue fabric, billowing, with the help of a hidden fan system, to imitate rolling waves. The fabric was also our method of eliminating as much ambient light as possible from the Convention Center's overhead lighting system and from the exhibits surrounding ours. We used movable lights to simulate the last rays of the sun's light reaching the floor of the sea. We also used rich blue LED uplighting to give a dark, shadowy effect to the set. The set design was based on the ruins of Greco-Roman architecture, inspired by underwater photographs and graphic artwork.

While the set was being constructed and designers and volunteers were being embraced, Kris set to work building all of the denizens of the deep. During a one-month period she created each of the six mythological mermen and mermaids and the two twelve-foot long sea horses that were to be chariot bearers for Neptune. The local big box hardware store became her best friend that month. Steel pipes, PVC, wood, screws, nails, adhesives, chicken wire, fencing, cable ties, and shelf liners, along with hammers, drills, electric saws, and any tool to finish the job were her instruments that month. Creating a bridal bouquet or a boutonniere became a welcome break as the weeks before the show drew shorter.

The Flower Show is truly a designer's challenge and accomplishment all rolled into one project.

—Corey Harbour

The on site design of this particular set was intense. Thousands of stems of roses, carnations, statice, asters, foliage, and branches were used to recreate the imaginings of a coral reef. Hundreds of stems of large green cordyline (Ti) leaves were used to give the appearance of swaying 10 to 15-foot tall kelp. We used heavy, steel-plated bases with welded thin steel rods as armatures. The Ti was then glued back-to-back with a floral adhesive for the final design. The mercreatures themselves had been heavily researched; blueprints and floral recipes had been honed. The designers were all here and work was about to commence – STOP!

Everything we planned, each detail was put on hold! We arrived with our set seven days before the show was to begin and now it was four days later and nothing had begun. You strategize and organize to make the process as smooth as possible. You prepare multiple "what if?" scenarios, but sometimes you face a challenge that is beyond your control. As exhibitors around us were building, planting, and designing, we sat on chairs with coffee and hot chocolates trying to keep warm in that cold, cold hall just meters from the open, enormous loading dock doors.

Hundreds of yards of fabric needed to be laid across the rigging and then pinned together to insure that no light bled through. We had calculated one half of a day to complete. We were at the mercy of the schedules of the work crews assigned to our rigging, and it took them two full days to finish the project and a third day to bring in the hydraulic cranes to raise the "underwater ceiling" into place. Finally, we can get to work – NO – not yet? The electricians and lighting technicians were also waiting their turn to complete their assignments. The show opens for judging at 7 a.m. on Saturday morning – it was now late on Wednesday afternoon. The day ended with our set finally being raised and the Kris-created mersculptures in their place. Time to start fresh on Thursday morning!

Friday arrived and we were finally able to start shoveling the two tons, 4,000 pounds, of recycled tires into the set. We had been waiting all week for the product to be brought across the expanse of the back halls and on to the show floor. The mulch had been delivered two weeks before, but was inaccessibly lodged behind thousands of pounds of stone block borders waiting for its release to us. We arrived Friday morning to the set and it was there...and it was the wrong color: it was green! Panic, frantic phone calls, and a long day of waiting finally brought a truck across multiple states with our correct, blue-colored rubber mulch. Down-to-the-wire is a term you do not want to experience in a situation like this. By the time we were able to finally get the two tons of mulch in place, complete the designs, and get the lighting set it was 6 a.m. – one hour before judging was to begin!

> *There are years where it all goes perfect. The stars seem to align and you are golden. Then there are times when it all seems like it's going haywire; nothing works according to plan. The beauty of design is the process, whether it is perfect or flawed. It teaches us to be flexible...to see alternate solutions ...to solve problems and keep moving forward. The times you are challenged make you even more proud. You overcome the obstacles to complete your vision and leave that cold vast Convention Center with a sense of victory, regardless of who wins a ribbon.*
>
> —Kristine Kratt

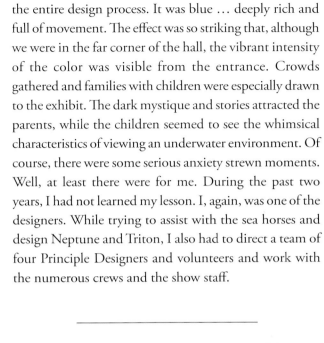

We did it! We somehow managed to actually complete the entire design process. It was blue … deeply rich and full of movement. The effect was so striking that, although we were in the far corner of the hall, the vibrant intensity of the color was visible from the entrance. Crowds gathered and families with children were especially drawn to the exhibit. The dark mystique and stories attracted the parents, while the children seemed to see the whimsical characteristics of viewing an underwater environment. Of course, there were some serious anxiety strewn moments. Well, at least there were for me. During the past two years, I had not learned my lesson. I, again, was one of the designers. While trying to assist with the sea horses and design Neptune and Triton, I also had to direct a team of four Principle Designers and volunteers and work with the numerous crews and the show staff.

I had never experienced anything like it … In five days, I witnessed the Pennsylvania Convention Center grow from acres of cold steel and concrete … to the sweet smell of what seemed like a million flowers … A new opportunity, to assist, provide input and have hands-on experience … now I knew there was more to the flower world, and I was right in the middle of it. What an honor. I was called, invited … I knew I was in the midst of some designers much more skilled than myself, so sometimes I learned and assisted. Other times, I would be instructing other volunteers that were less skilled than I. It felt great to mentor and to be mentored.

—Adelaide Beth Linn

Taking the Flower Show Home

At the end of the previous year's Flower Show, Sam Lemheney, Senior Vice President for Shows and Events, asked me if we knew of any floral design company who might be interested in exhibiting at the Flower Show. He wanted to know if we specifically would put our company's name on the line with a recommendation. I had had the opportunity to freelance alongside Armas Koehler and Bailey Hale at a top design studio in Philadelphia. They had previous experience as freelance designers working at the Philadelphia Flower Show and for "Jazzed" we asked them to lend their talents as part of Schaffer Designs Principle Design Team. They had just started their own company and, when Sam made his inquiry, it was an easy answer. They were wholeheartedly endorsed. One year later, their company won *Best In Show*. Though it is never easy to not be the chosen-one, as self-appointed educators of floral design, it was a proud moment for us knowing that it was our recommendation that gave someone else an opportunity to shine.

Taking the Flower Show Home

INTERPRETATION

In the Flower Show Exhibit "Atlantis," the set was a true fusion of numerous materials, textures, and colors. For our tabletop depiction of the display, we have created a design with multiple components brought together to form the underwater scene. Like the ocean depths it portrays, this design offers endless combinations to create the colors and movement of a vibrant coral reef.

MATERIALS

4" x 40" Slim Rota glass cylinders
20-gauge florist wire
Design Master® Color Tool –
    Holiday Red spray paint
Flat wire, aluminum
Fresh sheet moss
Manzanita branches
OASIS® Deluxe 22" floral foam
    Maxlife™ mâché wreath
OASIS® floral adhesive, tube
Petholatus shells
Reclaimed ocean barnacles
Water Pearls, 150ml, blue (2 jars)

FLOWERS

Aspidistra, 'Milky Way'
Dianthus, orange (carnation)
Dendranthema x grandiflorum
    (pompon, yellow button)
Leucadendron, 'Winter Sunshine'
Leucospermum, pincushion protea
Rose, spray, orange 'Sashaba'

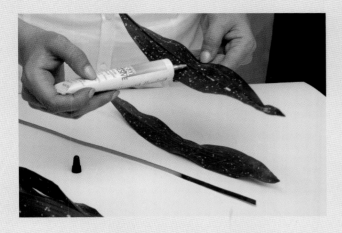

CONSTRUCTION

This design is a composite grouping of individual pieces. The final placements of all of its pieces are to be assembled in the location that it is to be displayed.

The first phase of this design should be started 24-hours in advance. Follow the instructions for the water pearls and allow them to soak overnight to fully absorb the water. After the full intake of water into the blue water pearls – distribute them into the 3 tall cylinder vases. Use red spray paint to color the pieces of manzanita. Fully soak the floral foam wreath and cover it with fresh sheet moss using 20-gauge florist wire as pins.

Start creating the "kelp" by removing the stems from the base of the 'Milky Way' aspidistra. Cut flat wire to length – plus an extra 2" for floral foam insertion. Lightly squeeze floral adhesive on the inside of each of the 2 pieces of foliage. Place one piece of aspidistra on the table – glue side up and lay the flat wire onto it. Place the second piece of aspidistra directly over the first piece and hold in place until glue is firmly secured. Repeat this procedure until each piece reaches the desired length. Add a wooden stick to the base of the flat wire by wrapping with floral tape. This will be used to insert into the floral foam wreath.

For the "yellow coral" cut the stems of the yellow button pompon 1-½"-2" below the head of the flower. Insert a piece of florist wire up and through the center of the stem – piercing the flower. Repeat this procedure until the desired number of flowers are on the wire.

Design the flowers into groupings around the wreath and place in its display area. Situate the 3 vases with water pearls inside the wreath. Position the kelp structures. After inserting the kelp, lightly bend the wired-foliage into slight waves to create the feeling of underwater motion. Add decorative accent items (manzanita, barnacles, seashells, etc.). To complete the "Atlantis" tabletop composition, add the pompon pieces into groupings of 2 or 3. Enjoy!

Chapter 4
POLAR FANTASY

PHS Award of Distinction
For the Second Highest Point Score

Emile H. Geschick Memorial Award
For Distinctive Orchid Display

Best Achievement Award
For Design of a Polar Fantasy

EXHIBITOR'S INTENT

Explain the overall design concept of the exhibit:
Where a frozen existence is ordinary, you're transported to a Polar Fantasy, where a Passport To The World can be expressed extraordinarily.

Explain the horticultural concept of the exhibit:
Where the expected is placed in an unexpected environment, using monochromatic flowers and other natural materials in an artistic expression of the juxtaposition of nature.

What impact do you want the exhibit to have on the visitor?
That the beauty of nature can be found in the most unexpected places and often in the most unexpected ways.

"Passport to the World" was the theme for the 2010 Flower Show. Exhibitors were given the opportunity to choose any place or idea in the world that would be ideal for representing flowers for their exhibits. We spent months without a solid concept for the project. In July 2009, long before Philadelphia's record-breaking 70+ inches of snow, I was driving Kris to the airport for a long flight with multiple layovers. Somehow, during this short 20-minute drive, Kris and I had our "eureka" moment. We decided to do something completely unexpected at the Flower Show, an environment where flowers didn't grow! – the polar ice caps. As we said our good-byes at the airport, Kris left the car obsessing over the idea. With her plane delayed in Philadelphia, we continued our conversation. As she landed at her first extended layover, our conversation started again. By the second stop, we were e-mailing Internet search engine findings back and forth to each other. By the time she arrived at her final destination, we had our concept. With our basic ideas in place, we soon began working on our inspiration boards. In mid-August, we met with Chris Kanienberg of Wish Painting and Sculpture and the ideas

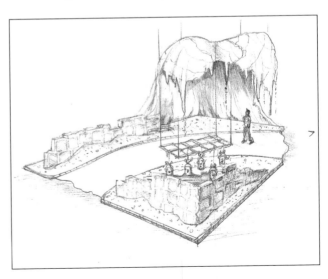

grew and grew. He discovered the trademarked darkness of Schaffer Designs in this stark, white-on-white, cold, ice-filled environment. Within a week, we had our first group of sketches from him ... and never looked back.

It took three years, but I had finally learned my lesson. I was not going to be a designer on site for "Polar Fantasy." The stress of trying to juggle so many hats had, in the past, caused me not to fully embrace and enjoy the process (not to mention the amount of patience that Kris needed to use to manage me). The answer was that no designer would be creating his or her own individual design. We were creating a complete environment and everyone would be working equally on the project at the Show. We decided to produce the entire project in advance of arriving on location. Kris took on the role of Lead Designer and I became the Director.

With this new design method in mind, Kris and I sent out invitational e-mails:

Hello Friends, We want to wish you Happy Holidays! OK – enough of the mushy stuff ... the opening of the Philadelphia Flower Show is in 3 months. We have once again been asked to be a Major Exhibitor at this year's Show (and the sucker that I am said – OF COURSE – and then Kris kicked me!) Themes have been decided upon, set construction is underway, flowers are being procured and, as usual, we find that we just could not do it so that it would be easy. So ... if you find yourself looking for a little adventure, a bit of hard work, and some real fun with a story to tell your friends, loved ones, Facebook friends and maybe even do a little self-promoting ... guess what? Do I have an opportunity for you?! No; that is not a question. YES; your opportunity awaits!

There was quite a bit more involved, including the design concepts and other details of the event, but it finished with "If you are interested in joining us for the fun, let me know ASAP!!!" This began a new era in how the Schaffer Designs process was to move forward. It opened up possibilities to bring in a greater number of designers, a way to share the experience with so many others who would not usually get the opportunity to explore this aspect of the floral industry.

My overall experience with the Philadelphia Flower Show has inspired me to be the best Floral Designer I can possibly be ... the moving works of art make me extremely proud to be in the floral industry.

—*Alisha Bell Simone*

Before we could gather together for the Flower Show setup, there were numerous in-depth design projects that needed attending to. Kris and I had created the massive armatures for our ice cave, but could not complete them on our own. The call went out! More e-mails, Internet postings, and phone calls brought in a fifteen-person team just four weeks prior to move-in day at the Convention Center. Three hundred bundles of white birch branch, ranging in size from 3-4 feet to 10-15 feet, were used to cover the galvanized steel fencing and chicken wired armatures that were waiting for them. They hand-tied more than 500 lightweight, white natural fiber sticks designed into a 25-foot long x 5-foot high x 3-foot wide floor armature that would hold hundreds of open-cut, white zantedeschia (commonly known as calla lilies) woven through it. Those two days were a major success! "Polar Fantasy" was being packed up and loaded into storage awaiting the big day!

We met at the American Institute of Floral Designers (AIFD) 2007 Symposium in Palm Dessert, California. Kris and Bill had stopped me to compliment my attempt at becoming AIFD accredited. How kind! Who was this funky couple who were saying they loved my designs? I loved them already. Two years later, I received an email and a follow-up phone call inviting ME to be a part of Polar Fantasy. I thought, "Should I? Can I?" Within seconds, I heard lyrics from Philadelphia Freedom blasting from my daughter's radio. That did it. I was going to Philadelphia.

—*Jodi Duncan*

We spent months developing our concept, experimenting with the layout and working on how we were going to create each design space. Perhaps the greatest challenge of all was how to use flowers that appear to be frozen solid, even with melting "ice" dripping from them? This piece was going to have REAL flowers frozen in REAL ice blocks brought in every morning and they would spend the day melting and wow-ing the crowds. We couldn't wait to see this floral art piece dead hung from the steel ceiling beams of the Pennsylvania Convention Center. "What? What do you mean that it isn't going to happen?" We found out that the company scheduled to do this had backed out and finding another company to do it was either impossible or, if they could do it, cost-prohibitive. Two weeks of valuable time were wasted searching for a vendor to work with us.

We were ready to give up on this whole aspect of the exhibit. It was now the second week of January and we had six weeks to go before move-in. We convened a designers meeting and agreed that if the Ice Pond had to go, it would be replaced with an inspiration from the polar-waste, crystalline architecture of a comic superhero: Superman's Fortress of Solitude. We were resigned to go ahead with the new plan when there was a major epiphany! The ice pond would be saved! It became better than the original plan. The "Fortress of Solitude" took shape as our frozen landscape behind the ice pond. It became the most talked about area of the exhibit. Like the saying goes, "If you get a lemon – make lemonade." We made frozen lemonade!

Cornerstone works, within my portfolio, have been created while working with Schaffer Designs. I will never forget how I felt when we turned on the pump to initiate the melting effects in the Polar Fantasy Ice Pond… it functioned absolutely perfect and that is totally unheard of in the Flower Show world.

—Christian Kanienberg, Wish
Painting & Sculpture

OK – a little secret. The ice blocks were found online as fish tanks. The treatment used for giving them that amazing frosted and dripping effect was a series of topical applications of a clear casting resin (also used for finishing bar tops). The pond above the installation was a 2" acrylic pond with water being snuck up one of the front legs by a heavy-duty pump, hidden in the water below. The vintage legs, ice-tongs, and all of the accessories were dipped in a white resin for that frozen finish. My favorite part of the exhibit was the hundreds of pin-holes drilled into the acrylic to give that all-day melting and dripping effect that the Flower Show crowds ooohed and ahhhed over. The open cut Dutch zantedeschia that were designed inside the fish tanks never had to be replaced. The dripping water continuously fed fresh water back into the pieces and they lasted ten full days submerged in the water-filled tanks.

The Philadelphia Flower Show was at the top of my bucket list … I have been forever changed just by being exposed to such professionalism and passion … It became more than just a mere job to be finished, but became about an overwhelming sense of pride, precise workmanship and unbridled love for the art that everyone produced …
—Andy Hopper

Taking the Flower Show Home

After months of agonizing over the logistics of turning our vision into a reality, we managed to produce the ice cave. It was approximately 6.7-7.65 meters (22-25 feet) in height. To give the snow-covered effect, the massive-welded steel structure that our prop master constructed was hung from the rafters and covered with three white parachutes. It took our entire team of designers and other volunteers to complete the placement of the 4,000 white dendrobium orchids used on the stalactites. It then took half of that team to lift those heavily weighted structures 25 feet in the air to connect them to the frame of the ice cave. The floor of the cave was filled with stalagmites jutting up to 7 feet into the air. To create the feeling of movement, over 300 feet of copper tubing sprayed with a white textural paint was woven through the design and then laced with 200 large white anthuriums. This part of the exhibit was so brightly lit in its stark white, frozen existence that it was visible from across the ten-acres of the exhibit hall floor.

The ice forest armature of zantedeschia and white fiber sticks encompassed a full day of work for Kristine Kratt and Jodi Duncan. The cut ends of the zantedeschia were individually hand-dipped in paraffin wax to seal in the water. They were then woven onto the armature, along with small pieces of plumosa foliage. Short strands of white string were tied to the armature. The structure was then meticulously coated by hand-pouring 100 pounds of paraffin wax, one cup at a time. The final effect was an amazing faux dripping of ice.

The only flowers that we had to replace for the duration of the show were the flowers nearest the public. Was the ice real, plastic, acrylic, glass, a block of wax? Were the flowers real, frozen, floating, melting, solid? The public found it hard to believe that the flowers were real.

We wanted them to be able to see the design up close, but it was just too tempting for a few thousand visitors whose over enthusiasm could not abide by the rule – Do Not Touch The Flowers! One particular comment that we overheard was "Oh my goodness! All of that wax will hurt the flowers." The average person going to the Flower Show doesn't know that we spent months testing the life expectancy of the product. The most common comment we heard was "I told you they weren't real." Even with all of the experimental touching of the flowers, we only had to replace 30 of the more than 200 flowers that were designed into this armature. If you consider the normal life expectancy of a flower in water and then take it out of water, dip it in wax at 144 degrees Fahrenheit and slowly drip more wax on to it after it is bound to an armature where 250,000+ people walk through within arm's reach, it was amazing that the rest of the flowers actually lasted the entire length of the show.

The first time I met Bill Schaffer was a year before he officially met me. It was 2010, and I made my annual pilgrimage to visit the flower show. The theme that year was Passport to the World. My friends and I meandered through the displays when we came upon Schaffer Designs' "Polar Fantasy." I was blown away by the unique display featuring callas frozen in blocks of ice. The stark white contrast to the rest of the show's growing displays attracted me to it. The display was a wildly different approach to anything I ever saw. I had to get a closer look.

I was enamored by the sight of hundreds of callas with a fresh sheen of ice. I needed to know what they used to create the frozen look. So being the curious girl that I am, I carefully reached to one of the back callas that was out of sight and plucked off a piece. "Wax!" I thought to myself, "Brilliant!" Just then, a gruff voice said "please don't touch the exhibit." Bill Schaffer had caught my proverbial hand in the cookie jar. I sheepishly apologized and took one of his business cards.

I immediately started cyber-stalking Schaffer Designs. In December of that year, I began my e-mail campaign to go to Philadelphia and volunteer. I was given the green light and, in February, I boarded a train. I didn't know a single person, but I was made to feel right at home from the moment I stepped into the convention hall. Bill and Kris gave me a welcome hug, a custom-designed scarf and set me to work. I arrived a stranger and left as family. That is how they operate. Beyond the brilliance, Bill and Kris are truly warm and generous people. The secret to their success might be their love and personality. They are the type of people you want to be around as much as possible. They make you want to be a better designer and better person. Bill and Kris changed my life, and I will be forever grateful for breaking off that piece of wax.

—*Melissa Huston*

In the end, we used 4,000 white dendrobium orchids, 4,000 white carnations, 100 stems of white phalaeonopsis orchids, 200 open cut white zantedeschia, 100 white hyacinth, 200 white nerine, 200 white Japanese sweet peas, 200 large white Hawaiian anthurium, 100 giant Japanese dahlias, plumosa, and 300+ bunches of painted white birch. In fact, we used close to 10,000 stems in the exhibit, all placed by over 25 designers and volunteers. The visitors loved the exhibit and, unbelievably, waited patiently in line for up to 40 minutes to walk through our set. The guests entered through ice-block walls inset with intermittent ice-like, sheer blocks for the curious to peer through during their wait.

During "Polar Fantasy," social media forever changed how Schaffer Designs communicated with our fellow designers. It changed how we communicated our Flower Show activities with the world. Social media was the source of our being discovered by the international floral community. It connected us to *Fusion Flowers Magazine* from Scotland and an international following was born.

As you sit at your desk, ponder too on how few people have the chance to experiment, to stretch their creativity — some never have. Here are you and your team with not only the chance but the certainty that you can and will not only bring a light into your own hearts through comradeship, friendship and the ability to be creative, but that — without ever knowing them — you will have done the same for others too.

—Alison Bradley, editor, *Fusion Flowers Magazine*

Taking the Flower Show Home

The creative process as well as the people were stimulating, exciting, amazing, and the world needed to know. I asked if I could share the process through social media. They said yes, so off I went, sharing behind the scenes images on Twitter and Facebook. A five-minute YouTube video titled *Polar Fantasy* went viral. I had found a niche with Team Schaffer.

—*Jodi Duncan*

Each year, as we begin our plans for the show, we start with a big idea that seems almost impossible to make happen. We hash it out, work and rework it, refine it, and make it overwhelmingly possible. This is how "Polar Fantasy" was born. We wanted something extreme. Something that pushed the boundaries of design, as well as the boundaries of what we can do with the flowers.

This was also the year "Team Schaffer" came into existence. Many hands had always helped with the exhibits in the past, but this year the group became an amazing, single entity. They moved from project to project, working together to complete each area with creative suggestions and beautiful attention to detail.

When the first stalactite was being raised up into the ice cave, the team stood below holding their breaths. As the massive structures clicked into place, they cheered and applauded. They were as much a part of this exhibit as we were at that point. Each had time and workmanship invested in this project and they were proud of the exhibit like it was their own.

So it had grown from Bill and I brainstorming from airport-to-airport, to some of the best floral talent in the world sharing their skills with us because they wanted to be a part of something bigger — something beyond just being a designer. In that freezing cold convention center, on our floor of white, beneath a ceiling of four-thousand white orchids, they made us a team.

—Kristine Kratt

ICE CAVE

Taking the Flower Show Home

Taking the Flower Show Home

THE ICE FOREST

Taking the Flower Show Home

THE ICE POND

Taking the Flower Show Home

Taking the Flower Show Home

Taking the Flower Show Home

Taking the Flower Show Home

INTERPRETATION

In the midst of one of the most colorful events in the world, "Polar Fantasy" was a stark, white-on-white, fantastical contrast. In this design, we revisit the icy-cold feeling of the exhibit. Though this particular design may seem best suited for the winter season – it is also a fun design for moments when the outdoor temperatures are soaring. The idea of flowers existing in such an environment requires that you use your imagination and let the art of the composition take you there. We are combining multiple elements from the exhibit into this single tabletop display. The chill of wintertime materializes in the flow of the frozen callas – as they emerge from the ice and snow blanket below.

MATERIALS

OASIS® UGlu™ adhesive/strips and dashes
Bud vases, square glass (20)
Fiber sticks, white (20)
Paraffin wax
Skillet
Measuring cup
Styrofoam™, shredded

FLOWERS

Zantedeschia, open cut, white (calla)

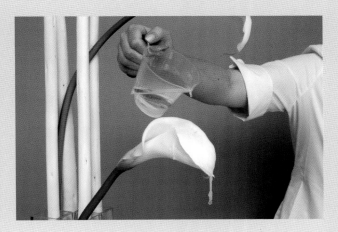

CONSTRUCTION

Use square bud vases for this arrangement. Before using new vases, properly clean them with soapy water to remove any residual oils. This is necessary for the adhesive strips to properly adhere to their surface.

Use adhesive dashes to connect the vases to each other. Place the dashes at the outer base and top of each of the vases to form the crystalline ice structure. For this particular variation, create five of these groupings. On the inside of each vase, place an adhesive dash to secure the fiber sticks. The fiber sticks are extremely buoyant and will not sink in the water but "bounce" upward. The adhesive dashes are to ensure your armature's shape. For larger fiber sticks, you will need to use a full adhesive strip to achieve greater surface coverage for bonding.

Cover your work area with a protective surface. In a large skillet; melt the paraffin wax. The recommended temperature setting is low. Insert two callas at different heights and lengths into 2 of the 4 vases in the group. Complete each of the 5 vase groupings separately. Move to final placement after this step is concluded. Using the measuring cup, slowly – very slowly – pour the wax over the calla until the dripping, stalactite is formed. Repeat this process on each flower and over their stems where desired.

Line the vase groupings on the table. Carefully (so as not to break the wax) adjust the callas into their final design space. Finally, add the shredded Styrofoam between the vases and around the base.

Taking the Flower Show Home

Chapter 5

AN AMERICAN IN PARIS

Pennsylvania Horticultural Society Flower Show Award For The *BEST IN SHOW* – Display Garden – Floral

Flower Show Award of SAF – Society of American Florists Award for Artistic Presentation of Flowers and Plants for Public Enjoyment.

Emile H. Geschick Memorial Award
For Distinctive Orchid Display

Best Achievement Award for the Incorporation of Rhythm in a Floral Display

EXHIBITOR'S INTENT

Explain the overall design concept of the exhibit:
Our inspiration is "An American in Paris;" our objective is to capture the movement of music and dance in dramatic lines, forms, and colors.
Explain the horticultural concept of the exhibit:
We have selected materials for their vivid color, unique forms, textural qualities and some new varieties to express the rhythm and movement of the film.
What impact do you want the exhibit to have on the visitor?
The visitor's experience of our floral interpretation of dance through film will leave them with a deeper appreciation of the connection of all art forms.

It was just 24 hours before the Show was to Preview for the Membership of the Pennsylvania Horticultural Society. Schaffer Designs teams were ahead of their schedules and everyone seemed to be in a groove. I remember circling the exhibit, looking for someone who needed guidance, someone waiting to be told his or her next assignment. There was nothing left for me to do but allow everyone to continue as they were. I decided to carry on with my walk when one of my design friends came running up to me looking like he was about to burst into tears. I knew it ... nothing could be this good! He grabbed my arm and said, "come with me, you have got to hear this!" He quickly led me to a woman, whom I later learned was Jocelyn McAdam. Jocelyn had been a docent for the Flower Show for many years and was touring all of the exhibits; learning the history of each design group and what they were creating for the early morning tours she would be giving each day of the show. By the time we were introduced, our entire design crew

had heard the story she was about to tell me. After we were introduced, she turned to the set with a look of wonder and said, "I am so happy; my father would be so proud." I asked her who her father was. She replied, "E. Preston Ames." It turns out that E. Preston Ames was famous. It was his vision that our entire set was based upon. He was the two-time Oscar-winning Art Director of *An American In Paris* in 1951 and *Gigi* in 1958, and was nominated an additional six times. Among the highlights of his career were *Brigadoon*, *The Unsinkable Molly Brown*, and *Earthquake*. As I was speaking with Jocelyn, I glanced to the side and saw the entire Schaffer Designs Team gathered with almost all of them crying! Tears of joy! What award, what accolade could be greater than to hear what we just were told?

12 MONTHS BEFORE …

I was envisioning islands of floral designs, each representing a scene from the movie *An American in Paris*. Lights and large video projections of the movie would go off and on, as they seemed to jump from one island of flowers to another just as Leslie Caron leapt into Gene Kelly's arms in so many of the dance sequences. This vision literally sprang into my mind the moment that I heard that the theme for the 2011 Philadelphia Flower Show was to be "Springtime in Paris." I was so excited about the idea that I told Sam Lemheney that same day. He liked the idea, but recommended caution about using film clips from the movie. After extensive research into the rights to the movie, we were given the green light to use what we needed. Of course, now that we had the go-ahead, there was a growing, acute awareness that this idea was too grand. The cost for the lighting, sound, carpentry,

carnival

city

cafe

large screen monitors, wiring, and rigging would have amounted to the entire budget for the Schaffer Designs Exhibit, plus the entire budget of each of our competitors combined. Next!

But the idea of using the movie as our muse was too enticing. We already had the okay to use the movie; we just had to formulate an idea to bring it all together. We thought a great deal about the dark, rich underbelly that Schaffer Designs had brought to the show and how it related to a 60-year-old musical that was ranked 68th on the American Film Institute's 1997 list of the 100 greatest American movies of all time and was ranked 9th on their Greatest Movie Musicals list in 2005. Silhouetted images of vintage movie cameras, lights, and director's chairs were discovered. That was it! The darkened soundstage of a period film set. A director's behind-the-scenes point-of-view.

Watching a musical, even a movie that you like, numerous times over a two-month period, rerunning the individual dance sequences in search of that perfect moment, well, it can be maddening. The songs have become permanently ingrained in our heads. We originally decided upon eight of those "moments," then dropped it to six and finally settled upon four individual, snapshot moments where the colors and movement of the set, actors and dancers could be captured with flowers. The guests would be able to view our selected designs in a 360-degree diorama of vignettes. We titled the four sets "Fountain," "Can-Can," "Carnival," and "Stairway." Considering that *An American In Paris* is a musical, 60-second audio and video clips of each of the scenes were to be played on a continuous loop throughout the Flower Show to give the attendees a connection between the two art forms.

The decor of the ballet will be its most distinguishing feature as to uniqueness and originality, for each individual scene will be done in the styles of different painters (Dufy, Renoir, Utrillo, Rousseau, Van Gogh, and Toulouse-Lautrec)...the ballet visually should reflect an artist's viewpoint and both the scenery and the costumes should be done as they were painted.... In essence, the entire ballet is a representation of a painter thinking about Paris.

—Ballet outline submitted by
Gene Kelly and Vincent Minnelli,
September 6, 1950

Taking the Flower Show Home

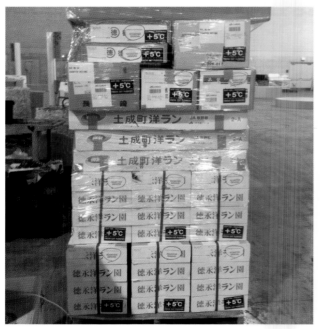

Taking the Flower Show Home

STAIRWAY

The first of our four vignettes was "Stairway." This design represented the Gershwin classic, "I'll build a Stairway To Paradise." The vignette was the smallest of our design spaces but its all pink décor with a black backdrop made it one of the most photographed sections of the exhibit. Hours upon hours were spent working the logistics of this design. We had originally found a group willing to donate an entire set of stairs used in a New Year's Day Parade, but when we went to look at it, we found it was bigger than our entire 1100 square foot space. What to do? Do we paint the staircase as a backdrop, suspend mechanical steps from the ceiling or from a wall, or use a trompe l'oeil painting? Should we have our own staircase built to fit?

We really wanted to create an impressionistic view of our stairway to paradise. The concept led us to answers for questions we had not even considered for our entire set. The stairs would be painted cutouts, playing with the viewer's perspective of depth and height!

Kris was working for a company that supplied the internally lit, opaque 3-foot and 4-foot tall vases. We designed acrylic structures to extend the designs up to 15 feet off of the ground. A floral foam wreath was placed at the top of each of the four vases for our flower insertions. The extensions became 4 x 2 foot galvanized-fencing-based designs with wooden crossbeams inserted to balance the pieces from above. The "lampshades" were wrapped in plastic window screening. Kris Kratt led the Design Team for this vignette (along with her multitude of other responsibilities). Our team made potpourri out of 3,000 pink carnations and spray-glued the petals to the four structures and secured them invisibly with fishing line. Sound easy? It took a crew of 3-4 people two full days to complete just the four lampshades. Somehow, the combination of how they were secured with the floral spray adhesive and the fluctuating temperatures of the Convention Center kept the design looking Day One fresh for the three days of setup and the nine days of the show. Twelve full days!

You realize that you are not designing for a typical exhibit that you are designing a complex art installation where every piece, flower and concept has been thought through to showcase creativity, innovation and the beauty of flowers.
—Marjorie Elzey

CARNIVAL

Our next vignette was held together by hundreds of tubes of floral adhesive! The scene was the first of three that represented the iconic, eighteen-minute ballet sequence at the end of the movie. We called it "Carnival." There were so many colors and dancers, so much movement of people and props in this sequence that it was almost impossible to select our freeze-frame moment. Then it leapt out of the screen. The brightly colored costumes of the chorus of dancing girls as they twirled and twirled in ever-widening then contracting circles was it. An elongated oval shaped steel ring was welded and hung almost 20 feet from the floor. The five dancing girls we were going to represent were made of bound birch branches fully covered in a canvas wrap. Though we had completely designed and sketched the final pieces and had created detailed recipes for each, we knew before the start of the week that it was going to be the most tedious of the design chores and needed someone whose personality was up for the task to keep this group excited and having fun. Our team leader for this vignette was Jodi Duncan. She led a crew of ten designers over a three-day period as they hand-glued, petal-by-petal, strand-by-strand, thousand of heads and petals of flowers and foliage to each of the 6 foot tall designs.

My experience with Schaffer Designs in 2011 was as exciting as an actual trip to Paris would be or to have worked on the film…It was incredible to assist in the construction and watch the space transform. I shall remember this experience for all times.
—Kimberly Nelson

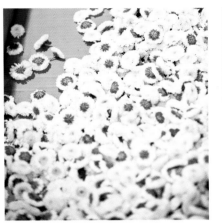
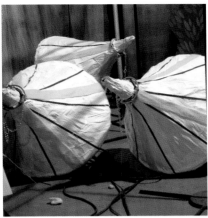

The Moulin Rouge, Jane Avril, Toulouse-Lautrec, and Gene Kelly's amazing interpretation of the famous dancer Chocolat were the inspiration for Schaffer Designs homage to the "Cancan."

Paper. 8,000 sheets of paper. How long does it take to pleat 8,000 sheets of paper and then hand-staple it into a fan shape? Oh, and then feed it through a custom-designed, handcrafted, chicken-wired armature and again staple the pieces together? The answer: it takes three full days with up to ten people! Kris dipped deep into her obsessive-compulsive, detail-oriented, crafty dark side and created this technique for us. Along with the 2,000 stems of white roses individually fed through the paper and water-tubed into swirling patterns, it allowed us to simulate the rich layers of ruffles that were made visible under our cancan dancers' skirts. The on site "Cancan" team was led by Bill Murphy, Sue Weisser and Tony Medlock, who oversaw the folding, stapling, rose cleaning, floral designing, and the manipulation of hundreds of stems of Jack Black Callas, Black Queen Anthuriums, and Black Cordyline foliage.

CANCAN

FOUNTAIN

Our grande finale was set around a Dufyesque fountain, reminiscent of the fountain in the Place de la Concorde in Paris. This vignette was titled the "Fountain." As the ballet closes, dancers from all of the previous scenes come together and begin twirling in continuous circles around the fountain. We wanted to create the feeling of the strength in that movement. This led us to the creation of a 75-foot steel spiraled structure that was hung more than 20 feet in the air. The spiral continued around our fountain until it was just 2 feet from the ground. This was a massive undertaking and Team Leader Andy Hopper had his work cut out for him. During the week, almost every designer was called

in to assist on the completion of this design. Dozens of multiple-sized Styrofoam discs were transformed into miniature circles of floral art as thousands of stems of Japanese Asplenium foliage were individually glued in circular patterns onto the disc. The pieces were then strapped onto the spiraling structure along with more than 20 grapevine-based wreath-like forms swirled with midollino and moss garlands. Gerry Gregg became our ladder guru, moving with the ease of a high wire artist, contorting himself to place hundreds of stems of flowers in their director-driven locations.

To give that point-of-view look of the director on a movie set, each of the vignettes was accented with

director's chairs and hand-made black foam core cutouts of vintage movie cameras, lights, and boom-microphones. We incorporated modern flat-screen televisions that had cutouts attached to them so they looked like vintage TV sets or monitors. The ground was strewn with hundreds of feet of electrical cables and each vignette had its own custom-designed roadbox that enclosed our modern ground lighting system. We surrounded the entire 1,100 square feet of the exhibit with black wooden sawhorse barricades to represent a live shoot and the area that the crowds could not cross. It was interesting to see the crowds notice the back-to-back scenes as the highest point of each vignette jutted above each scene.

Taking the Flower Show Home

I consider myself a self-appointed bodyguard of the Schaffer Design aesthetic. It is the responsibility of any designer worth their salt to have that sense of shared accountability with the final work.

—Christian Kanienberg,
Wish Painting & Sculpture

We really wanted this year to be special for the attendees. In years past, the biggest question we were consistently being asked was; "what flower is that?" We decided to incorporate a table on which we mounted vases to represent each stem of flower and foliage used in the entire exhibit. We listed their botanical names and origin. It was a groundbreaking year for us with the addition of our Japanese Flower Partner. We were able to show seven Japanese flower varieties that had not been used in the United States in an exhibit like this before and at least six others whose United States import status was limited to just a couple of U.S. markets.

"Fairies," "Jazzed," "Atlantis," and "Polar Fantasy" had all been leading up to the extravaganza of "An American in Paris." Thirty designers from all over the United States, multiple behind-the-scenes partners, and more set builders, riggers, carpenters, electricians and dock workers than I can count all came together to make it a truly successful year! The gathering of people created an overall experience that was different from those of previous years. Social media followers had us bombarded with requests to come to Philadelphia and be a part of the team. It seriously became a "first come, first serve" request line. We had a few people who were on our "must-have" radar, but the notoriety from social media and the press that we received had people locking in their spot early. We had the opportunity to put together a "floral dream team."

Never have I worked so hard, laughed so much, slept so little, and came away with such an undeniable sense of fulfillment!

—Lee Gallison

Design and creativity are such organic entities…always changing and reshaping where we go next with our imaginations. The evolution of an idea for an exhibit of this size takes many brains and, in the end, many hands. Part of the process in our personal design growth has been to learn when to take our own hands off of the work and let the team do what they came here to do. Create our vision.

—Kristine Kratt

The *Schaffer Designs Newsletter* announced the advance design days and within a single day we had all three weekends booked with some designers driving in from hundreds of miles away just to assist with the construction phases of our armature and prop building. Along with the advance design days there were numerous long evenings that we spent working with our close friend Alfred Price, as we devised and constructed props big and small for the set.

When we met for prep work, a few weeks before installation, Bill and Kris went over their visions and concepts with us. Although I tried, I couldn't quite wrap my mind around it. However, I knew the exhibit was in good hands, so I just did what I could to bring the pieces to life… leave it to Bill & Kris to "think outside the bloom!"

—*Renee Tucci*

The big day had arrived. Everyone knew that we had given it the best that we could. The friendships that had rooted and grown in such a short time were richly rewarding. The team gathered around the exhibit as we waited for word…the word. Nothing. Attendees of the show clamored for pictures around the set. We listened to people saying how much they enjoyed it. We waited. About three hours into the wait the first of 3 awards would be brought to the exhibit, but we still waited to find out who would be awarded the "Big One." One-by-one our team of friends began departing for the airport as their journey home began. As the announcements that the show would be closing in 15 minutes, then 10 minutes, then 5 minutes were announced…our hearts sank. We looked into the faces of those remaining and just wanted an answer for them. We didn't want to send them home without knowing. The announcement for the closing of the show came…nothing; moments later my cell phone rang. It was Sam Lemheney asking "how is everything going?" "have you been able to get any rest?" "how was the day for you?" I don't remember how he said what immediately followed, but I heard the word "unanimous." He said, "Congratulations, you won Best in Show." He said something about 106 points, perfect score, and extra credit. He said, "the judges could find nothing wrong!" I looked up and everyone was staring at me. I don't remember hanging up; I just remember the most wonderful group hug ever!

The Philadelphia Flower Show is a showcase for the best work in floral design, and Schaffer Designs has deserved its numerous honors as "Best in Show."

—*Drew Becher, President of the Pennsylvania Horticultural Society*

We won! Our team went home and, like a big party for a newborn baby's homecoming when all of the guests leave, we stood there alone with our baby. An over-scaled, 1,100 square foot baby, and we had over 12,000 stems of diapers to change for the next eight days.

When will it end? lolololololololololol OMG! I went to just start cleaning as much of the "rotting" as I could and everything just started falling apart. OY! By that point – well, might as well keep going. The big Cancan girl is completely refreshed – touch-up tonight on the other two. Kris has magically brought the Carnival girls back to life for the second half of the show. The Fountain has had many nights on a ladder of water tube changes and the gloriosa finally went yesterday … MAKEUP! The Stairway finally had a wreath refresh. All of the sweet pea kept burning up so we replaced them with the Japanese Phalaeonopsis and it is looking better than ever. The lampshades look better every day! Note to self; what takes 30 people, 3 full days to design and 100s of hours to construct – CANNOT be easily maintained by 2! It is 2 a.m. – just finishing. Back at 7 a.m. to turn it on and light it up. All morning at work, a demonstration at 3:30 p.m. and massive maintenance again Thursday night, but it looks GREAT!"

—From a Facebook posting by Bill Schaffer, March 10, 2011

Taking the Flower Show Home

Taking the Flower Show Home

Taking the Flower Show Home

INTERPRETATION

Choosing which of the uniquely blueprinted vignettes to illustrate has made this our most difficult selection. There were just too many ideas for each of the four areas of the exhibit. In the end, we realized that during that particular Flower Show, the majority of "how did you do that?" questions from the attendees were about the cancan. We wanted to offer the "How-To" for the "Cancan" segment, but also blend in the color of the most photographed vignette, "I'll Build a Stairway To Paradise." Blending the two presents the perfect way to create a vintage-inspired design. The portrayal of the cancan girls in a tabletop design gives the opportunity to create an armature that can be used many times.

MATERIALS

Book, recycled pages
Chicken wire
OASIS® standard foam brick
Stapler and staples
Tray, ceramic, rectangular

FLOWERS

Rosa, 'Sahara'
Rosa, spray, pink majolica

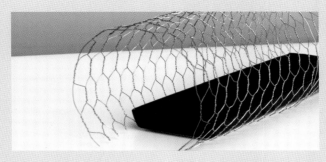

Using an older, recycled or damaged book will give you the dog-eared, yellowing edges for this vintage look (if unavailable, newer pages or paper is also an option). Prepare the pages in advance of starting the design. Loosely fold the pages into triangular shapes and staple the pointed end to hold the appearance. Put 2, 3 or 4 of the individual triangular pages through the chicken wire. From inside the rounded armature, staple their ends together. By stapling, you insure that they will not be displaced or fall out of the armature. As you complete each group, "fluff" the paper so that the printing is visible. Repeat this process until the chicken wire form is full. "Full" does not mean that you have to fill every single hole in the chicken wire. As you begin to place more and more of these page groupings into the armature, you will note that the space appears to be filled without using every opening. *Caution:* since the composition is being made with paper, make sure that the triangular pages that you are creating do not touch the water source.

Begin flower insertions. In the sample design, we played with using floral groupings. The groupings are patterned through the design to create the soft lines. Using the 'Sahara' roses and the pink majolica spray roses, mixed with the older pages, gave us the vintage look and feel.

Option: though more time consuming, this design can be made without the container. Each rose stem inserted through the chicken wire can have an individual water tube filled with water and inserted onto the freshly cut stem. In the sample design, we used 45 stems of roses – this would mean that you would need 45 water tubes. This option allows for greater mobility of the design. If you proceed with this option, make sure that the stems are long enough so that the water tubes do not come in contact with the paper. If so, the paper would quickly wick the water into itself and spread through the surrounding pages.

CONSTRUCTION

Start this project by picking a container. The look of the container is not important because the aesthetic value of it will not be visible in the completed arrangement. The container's dimension will dictate the size and shape of the design. The flower stems will be entering the floral foam at steep radial angles, therefore the container should be low and the foam easily accessible. Once you have chosen your container, line it with wet, fully saturated floral foam. Keep the floral foam low in the container. Its main function is as a water source and to secure a place for each of the stem insertions. Using wire cutters, cut the chicken wire to fit over the length of the container; keep in mind that the length of the stems and the angle that is needed to easily insert the stems into the floral foam dictates the measure of the chicken wire past the span of the container.

Chapter 6
PELE – GODDESS OF FIRE

Pennsylvania Horticultural Society Flower Show Award
BEST IN SHOW – Display Garden – Floral

Flower Show Award of SAF
Society of American Florists Flower Show Award
for Artistic Presentation of Flowers and Plants
for Public Enjoyment

EXHIBITOR'S INTENT

Explain the overall design concept of the exhibit:
The Epic Struggle – Man vs. Nature. Man's raw, unfinished industrial constructs vs. Nature's destructive beauty as flowing lava and its explosive forces triumph.

Explain the horticultural concept of the exhibit:
Rich colors, unique forms and textural qualities of traditional and new tropical varieties are displayed on geometric armatures interpreting Hawaii's volcanic origins and continuing transformation.

What impact do you want the exhibit to have on the visitor?
To feel they have been transported to a lava flow. To appreciate how floral design can blend flowers with unexpected, architectural and geometric materials.

The interest that the public displayed for the table of cut flower specimens that we worked into Schaffer Designs' 2011 exhibit, "An American In Paris," gave us an idea. We started sketching a multi-media, educational display that would take viewers on a journey from the farms to the Flower Show. An opportunity to do a floral design program on Kaua'i came from a group of Hawaiian growers who were touring the 2011 Flower Show. Of course, we said yes and proceeded to contact a group of growers and wholesalers on Kaua'i and the "Big Island" to visit for our homework. We secured numerous videos from the different farms. The intention was to design multiple-floral, color-grouped tiki huts that the visitor would walk through, while viewing videos from the growers. "Live" design demonstrations throughout the show were being planned for inside the exhibit. The excitement to present this objective to the decision-

makers at the Flower Show was building. Finally, the day arrived. Uh-oh! In their opinion, it seemed too educational and would put us in a different category of exhibitors. We were leaving for Hawaii in just a week!

Our plans were already made! What were we to do? We headed to Hawaii with an open mind; hoping the islands would present to us an idea on the proverbial "silver platter."

Tropical flowers, tropical colors, sand, sea, hula, leis…having spent the first few days on the Big Island, we realized that we needed to dig deeper for our inspiration, to do something unexpected. The vistas were amazing; everything about Hawaii is amazing, but, no matter where you look there is an ever-present reminder of how the Hawaiian Islands were formed: volcanoes. During a tour of the Halemaumau crater in the Kilauea Volcano, our National Parks Tour Guide told the tragic story of the goddess Pele and her true love, a young chief named Lohiau. A true "lightbulb" moment! Now, we didn't want to do a child's science project of plaster, baking soda and vinegar spewing forth its bubbly, fizzy magma mess. We wanted to represent the power of earth's creativity. After returning home, additional online research led us to amazing images and inspiration. Not the actual volcano, but lava, and through lava, "Pele – The Goddess of Fire."

The Philadelphia Flower Show is a serious event for the City of Philadelphia. It generates over 60 million U.S. dollars of revenue for the city. Over one-quarter of a million attendees from around the world come to see

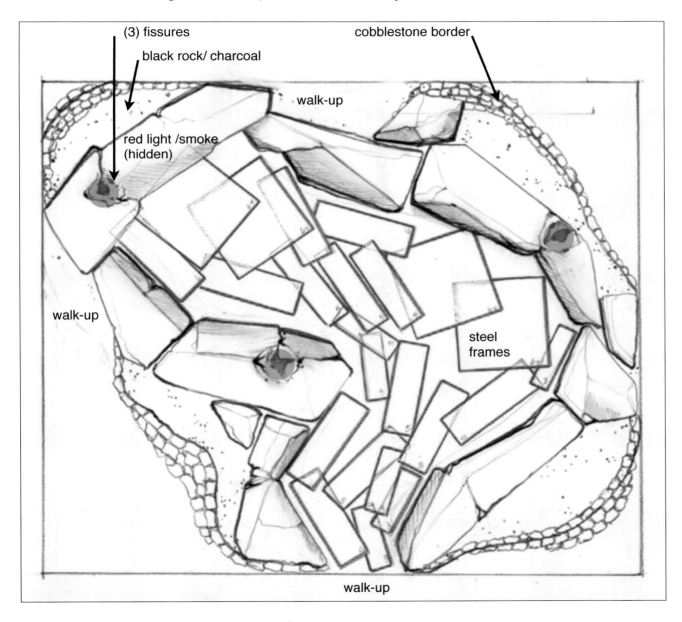

what you have created. It is a media circus. The pressure was on to equal, if not top, our 2011 *Best in Show* honors. Now, we'll admit, winning the top award is always in the back of our minds, but creating *wow* is first and foremost. This year, 30 designers from around the United States and the United Kingdom were invited. These designers came here at their own expense. Knowing this, we knew we had to offer them a seriously challenging project that all involved would benefit from.

This display had a mesmerizing effect on everyone as we worked. On the last day of the set up, everyone continuously would just take a step back — entranced by the magic that was Pele. Had this goddess of fire set her spell over all of us? Yes she did!
—David Hamilton

The creative process, and all that it entails, is unique to every artist. The process is never an easy one, but it does take you on a journey. In creating an exhibit of this size, choosing the flowers becomes the final phase. Like choosing a container for a table design, the vessel itself often dictates the direction of the designer. The Schaffer Designs Exhibit is almost 1100 square feet or just over 100 square meters: it is a big container! Deep rich colors, unique forms, and textural qualities of

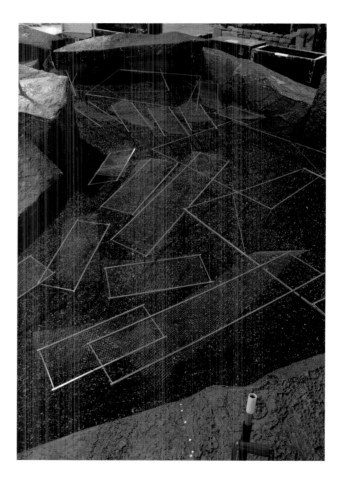

Taking the Flower Show Home

traditional and new tropical flower varieties displayed on geometric armatures were chosen interpret Hawaii's volcanic origins and continuous transformation. The preparations for the blueprinting of the exhibit took almost four months to complete. Gathering Partners for the requisition of so many materials took almost six months. To build the set from start to finish took almost one full month. Our move-in schedule and on site completion of the set took two days. The Flower Design Team worked four full days on site to complete the entire design process.

Bill and Kris made sure that Pele had strong bones, and then set her free to be fleshed out by the contributions of so many talented, devoted designers. There was nothing more important to any of us than to see this transformed into the amazing piece of art it became!
—Lee Gallison

Our first brainstorming session with our set designer was during a dinner. The table was cleared and all of our glasses and stemware were used to show the envisioned layout of the exhibit. We were using black napkins... perfect! They were placed over the glasses to represent the basalt – black lava rock. The overall shape of the exhibit was, pardon the pun, set in stone – or, in this case, plastic panels, vacuum-formed under high heat then machine-pressed, cooled, and dyed to give it its textural finish. They were then reheated and hand formed over massive, custom-built steel armatures and finished with raw steel rivets).

We had already decided to focus upon the epic struggle of man versus nature: man's raw, unfinished industrial constructs versus nature's destructive beauty as flowing lava and its explosive forces triumph. Each component of the project could be considered a completed design but it was the unity of the pieces that would create the true single vision, a complete floral environment. With that in mind, we wanted to truly showcase the "man-made" set and the floral armatures. We left the legs of the rock formations visible and also exposed the 2,000+ rivets. The idea for the lava flow was a surreal, rhythmic design. Using a series of visible,

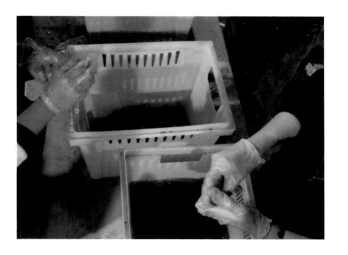

Taking the Flower Show Home

red-painted, steel frames with galvanized caging as the armature, the team fed over 1,000 red Hawaiian anthurium through the structures and into water tubes. This created the basic shape of our lava flow. We added Japanese Oncidium obrizatum to give the lava a true feeling of movement through the exhibit. To complete the lava flow, we positioned almost 300 Heliconia psittacorum x to represent the ever-present, mini-explosions of lava spouting from its surface.

Volcanoes are dangerous even when they are on the show floor of the Pennsylvania Convention Center. Curled up on the floor, under the set's framework, placing anthurium in the grids would seem to be a safe and serene endeavor … or so I thought. A forklift driver took a corner too sharp and BOOM! It hit the set and the entire structure shifted 8 inches with me hunkered down inside. It scared me and brought a whole new meaning to "taking one for the team."

—*Jodi Duncan*

We challenged our set designer to fabricate structures that would allow us to recreate the imaginings of exploding fissures with their hot magma shooting out of the earth. He came up with the idea of welding steel to form the bases and framework that allowed the on site designers to build three individual armatures scaling up to 23 feet each (7.01 meters). To create these armatures, we used natural red fiber sticks and over 700 upright and hanging mixed varieties of Hawaiian and South

Taking the Flower Show Home

American Heliconia. Exploding out of the top of the structures were more than 200 stems of Japanese Red Mitsato Gloriosa. These designs were each assigned a Team Leader and two assistants and each required almost two full days to complete. These designs were nonstop ladder work and were finally completed when nearly invisible cables were tied to the internal framework and then lifted on cherry-pickers and attached to the Convention Center's support beams to add stability to the design – just in case an overenthusiastic visitor decided to scale them … seriously!

Not every planned element works as well in life as on paper. The advantage of a creative mind is its ability to adapt and create beyond the plan.
—*Janet Frye*

I like to think of what we do for these installations as our version of Floral Theater™: interactive, bold, edgy, pushing boundaries of traditional displays to a level of performance art. To help create this interactive approach to the exhibit, we placed two individual walk-up areas. The guests walked over liquid plasma tiles resembling molten lava. The floor was covered with 3,000 pounds (1.36 metric tons) of crumbled, recycled tires – to resemble fallen ash. To create the feel of glowing fire, we installed 30 ground LEDs pulsating through the red/orange/yellow spectrums. Installed in the fissure designs were over 100 glass drops filled with red dyed water to enhance the reflective value of the additional lighting that we installed to uplight the individual armatures.

To top off the interactive experience, a fog-machine was installed to sporadically fill the area with a steamy, smoky mist. Our last interactive element was a display of each individual flower placed along with its botanical name to give the public an added educational connection to the exhibit.

This year I had the opportunity to join Schaffer Designs to fulfill one of the things on my floral bucket list. I always dreamed of being part of the team, now my life is changed forever. The flower show was the most amazing floral event I have ever seen...the friendships that are created while working together are priceless. My experience has inspired me to spread the word...Now my bucket list has a return trip.

—Sandy Schroeck

Two weeks before the Show was to open, something seemed to be missing. We couldn't figure out what it was. We decided to reach out to our design team for help. In an e-mail we explained our dilemma. We told them what we thought was needed and asked them for advice on how to make it happen. Piecing together ideas from each of their responses allowed us to come up with our field of burnt life. Repeating the steel frames that created the lava flow, we created six more, painted them black, and stood them upright with oversized, charred wood pieces inside. The floral elements were hanging "fuzzy" heliconia and 1,000 black cordyline with the spine removed and each side folded and pierced onto steel poles. Okay, this is a very elegant aspect of the design process that sounds easy. It is not! Carefully cutting out the spine of each and every stem of foliage and then individually folding each half (that's 2,000 halves) and skewering it into position is severely time-consuming. With 6-8 people gathered around a table, camaraderie and laughter enabled the team to complete this project in just under one full day. This final phase of the overall design connected the outside of the display to the inside. It was the final piece to the one-year puzzle that created "Pele – Goddess of Fire."

Having the privilege to design on a major exhibit each year gives me such pride in what I do. I have been able to share my passion with people, many who I will never meet but have been able to make a lasting impression on. Hopefully one that they will carry with them forever.

—Marjorie Elzey

"Best In Show" was much sweeter this year for so many reasons, the first of which was that for the first time ever we had our entire Principle Design Team present when the trophy was brought to the exhibit to share the experience with us. Second, on-hand was Schaffer Designs' friend Kelly Mace, who represents our most loyal partner during our entire six-year involvement with the Flower Show. Also present were representatives from the media. Last, but not least, the honor kicked off the beginning of our wedding week. Yes, Kris and I were getting married!

Taking the Flower Show Home

Taking the Flower Show Home

Taking the Flower Show Home

Taking the Flower Show Home

Taking the Flower Show Home

Taking the Flower Show Home

Taking the Flower Show Home

Taking the Flower Show Home

INTERPRETATION

At first glance this is a basic layered hedge design. As you look closer, you find a detailed patterning of foliage that is used to create the richest layer of the arrangement. The overall design is completely inspired by our 2012 Philadelphia Flower Show exhibit. It utilizes numerous elements from the original exhibit to form this tabletop rendition. The black container represents the basalt rock formations from around the set, while the black deco pebbles harken to the feel of the recycled tire-mulch used in the exhibit to portray the fallen ash. The folded foliage is a miniature version of the thousands of pieces displayed in the original version. The carnations symbolize the lava flow and the heliconia psittacorum assumes the role of the hot molten lava as it erupts and spouts forth from the volcano and surrounding fissures. The only element we didn't add here would be the smoke/steam effect that we used during the Show (we wish we would have thought of that!).

MATERIALS

Container, low, square metal – black
Design Master® Color Tool – flat black
OASIS® standard foam bricks (2)
Pebbles, deco black
Wood stakes, 18"

FLOWERS

Cordyline fruticosa, large, black 'Ti'
Dianthus, red (carnation)
Heliconia psittacorum, 'Fire Opal'

CONSTRUCTION

As advance preparation for this design, spray paint the wooden sticks black. Fully soak the floral foam in water. Cut floral foam ¼" to ½" below the open surface of the container. Fill the container with the floral foam. Evenly spread the black deco pebbles over the surface of the floral foam, completely covering it.

Using a knife, remove the spine of the black cordyline foliage. Pictured in this configuration there are 25 skewers of folded cordyline foliage. Each skewer needs 5-6 pieces of the folded foliage. The quantity required would depend upon the density you wish to display in your design. In this design, you will need a minimum of 63 stems of foliage and a maximum of 75 stems. Individually fold each half of foliage (do not crease the folds). Using your knife; pierce each folded portion completely through, then proceed to skewer each piece onto the black-painted wooden stake (5 or 6 per stake).

After the stake contains all of its allotted foliage, open up/spread out the folded pieces to cover the stake in an accordion-like fashion. Leave enough of the pointed end of the wooden stake clear to fully insert into the floral foam. Create even rows of the folded foliage stakes throughout the container.

Feed the carnations through the design and fully insert each one into the floral foam. *Tip:* the carnations can all be cut to the same length in advance. Measure the distance from the base of the insertion point to the base of the carnation so that just the head of the flower is visible above the skewers of foliage. The final step is to insert the Heliconia psittacorum to give the feeling of erupting lava.

THE WEDDING

On Wednesday, July 7, 2011, immediately following our presentation at the American Institute of Floral Designers National Symposium in San Francisco, California, Bill asked me to marry him. In front of almost 900 people. I was so surprised, I never actually spoke the word "yes." I did, of course, cry and nod and hug him and put on his beautiful ring. It was a gift of a moment that I would never forget the rest of my life.

This is us. Surprises and twists. The expression of our feelings for each other is obvious when we create together. The passion for everything we do is big, and sharing it just comes naturally. Everyone told us, "you'll never be able to top that!" Well, this is how we topped it!

During a meeting for the Flower Show, in early December 2011, we were informed that each day of the show would feature a different theme. One of the days was to be called Wedding Wednesday. One of the Design Studio's Committee Chairs turned to me and said, "Hey Bill — didn't you just get engaged?" I was being set up. The next thing you know everyone at the table was saying "wouldn't it be wonderful" to be married at the Flower Show! They said, "No one was ever married 'Live' at the Flower Show." I sat there stunned — thinking — Oh, Great! Kris is never going to agree to this. Then they said, "what if we could send you to Hawaii for your honeymoon?" Seriously?! OK, now this could be interesting.

—Bill Schaffer

Taking the Flower Show Home

Fast forward to January 2012. In the midst of a busy month of travel, design shows, and exhibit preparations, the Flower Show called and wanted us to be married in the middle of the crowd during the evening hours of March 7th. We didn't think it was really going to happen. I was terrified. Not because of the crowd. Because I had no dress, no shoes, no invitations, and no time. It was less than two months until "Wedding Wednesday."

With the love and kindness we already knew was in the hearts of our floral friends, three of the best offered to take a break and help me find a dress. I highly recommend bringing several of the best designers you know to help dress you for an occasion such as getting married in front of 10,000 people. They were not going to let me look bad! Within 3 hours of marathon dress selection, the vote was unanimous, and we had the dress sent on its way to Philly. Relief!

As the day fast approached and our exhibit was being created, there were an overwhelming myriad of newspaper articles and television interviews appearing about our upcoming exhibit and our "big day"... Two florists saying "I do" in the middle of the largest flower show in the world was creating quite a stir.

The groom had no shoes. My planner background kicked into high gear as we escaped the show long enough to find the perfect shoes and pick up everyone's tuxes. Sending photos back to the bride for approval, we had a productive day and returned with a groom who was camera-ready for his "I do."

—*Jodi Duncan*

Taking the Flower Show Home

Lighting

Eventions
Productions

I always felt that I learn so much from life's chances to give of my time and to learn and share from others who have this same quest. I have helped out at the Philly Flower Show for several years and always have walked away with a sense of WOW ... Not only do I meet great people who are now friends, but I came to know two people who give so much of themselves and the electricity that fuels my creativity. I have worked for a lot of designers who take all the credit, while you do most of the work, but I love working this show because it is all about the design and EVERYONE is encouraged to take credit. I mentioned a few years ago that I thought Kris and Bill had a perfect marriage of ideas, not knowing they have a perfect marriage of spirit. I walk away feeling a part of something very special. A union of spirit, friendship, art, childlike laughter. I would do it again and again. It's like the best ride at the amusement park! I admire and love the gifts that I come away with and the opportunity to work with Kris and Bill. There is nothing better."

—*Anne Gallagher*

I had never imagined being married in a setting like that. I had never dreamed of walking in a wedding gown through a massive crowd of people who wanted to share a glimpse of our floral lives becoming joined forever beneath a 25-foot waterfall in a tropical flower wonderland. As we finished the Schaffer Designs exhibit, we could finally turn to the details of the wedding just days away. So much to do ... and the flowers needed to be amazing. I wanted to make my own bouquet ... I had a vision of what it should be, and also for the other personal flowers and boutonnieres. Bill agreed and let me go for it. This was truly one of those times that despite how much we wanted to create all of the designs ourselves, there was no way it was going to happen without help. Enter Team Schaffer. Our fantastic friends stayed for the wedding and made sure everything was designed and perfectly placed for the reception.

When we finally exchanged rings and "I do's," we looked out onto a sea of thousands of people ... family and friends and Flower Show attendees who were now a part of our lives forever. It was a huge moment, shared in a big way, in a place that started it all for us. We had come full circle from the days of trees with Fairie shoes, to a fiery lava exhibit that ignited the hearts of a lot of people as a newly married floral couple stood alongside it to cut their wedding cake. To have shared the culmination of it all with those that we love and with happy strangers who love flowers made the experience beyond amazing.

The passion for all that we do is who we are, and the passion we have for each other makes anything possible, and on that special day at the Philadelphia Flower Show, we had never more truly felt the words "BEST IN SHOW."

See you at the Flower Show...

AUTHORS

BILL SCHAFFER AIFD, AAF, PFCI

As a successful third generation floral designer, Bill grew up in the floral industry. Founded in 1925, Bill's family's shop in Philadelphia, Pennsylvania, was attached to the family home. From sweeping the floors and selling flowers and plants as a kid, to delivering and then designing flowers after school, Bill has been given a lifelong passion for flowers and floral design.

With a successful reputation preceding him, Bill ventured out as a freelancer and quickly became in demand as a designer and consultant. He has developed considerable expertise in delivering informative and instructional workshops on floral design. Bill is much in demand as a speaker and educator ranging from wholesale shows, to national floral events, to garden club presentations.

Bill is the Co-Owner of Schaffer Designs, Floral Design Services based in Philadelphia, Pennsylvania. He has an award-winning reputation with multiple "Best In Show" honors at the Philadelphia Flower Show along with numerous other awards and honors over the past six years. His exceptional floral designs have been featured in regional, national, and international magazines, television interviews, and numerous websites and blogs.

Bill makes his home in Philadelphia with his wife Kristine Kratt.

KRISTINE KRATT AIFD, PFCI

Kristine Kratt's design education and international travel brings together her expertise in color, marketing, trends, and the principles and elements of design. Her presentations at national conventions, state floral associations, and national garden clubs focus on modern, trend-driven designs. She specifically addresses generational-target marketing for millennial consumers.

Kristine cultivated her floral career in San Francisco, California, and then moved to Dallas, Texas, where she began specializing in permanent botanicals, merchandising, and showroom installations. Expanding her design influence, she started working in overseas product development. Since that time, she has quickly become a diverse contributor within the floral industry, extending into special event design, design shows, workshops, national and international design publications, and televised interviews.

Kristine is co-owner of Schaffer Designs and co-creator of the multiple-award winning Schaffer Designs exhibits at the Philadelphia Flower Show. She resides in Philadelphia with her husband, Bill Schaffer. Kratt constantly furthers her personal design knowledge, and has traveled throughout the U.S., Europe, and Asia to participate in design projects. Kris is constantly sharing education and inspiration within the floral industry.

Taking the Flower Show Home

SCHAFFER DESIGNS TEAM

Wendy Andrade NDSF, FBFA, AIFD – 2012

Alisha Bell Simone AIFD – 2010

Kristie Lynn Borchick – 2010

Michael Boskey AIFD – 2007

Kelly Buck – 2008

Michael Brody AIFD – 2010, 2012

Monika Capozzi – 2011, 2012

Nick Codd – 2011, 2012

Rick Cuneo AIFD – 2011

Jodi Duncan AIFD – 2010, 2011, 2012

Ted Donaghy AIFD – 2007

Marjorie Elzey – 2010, 2011, 2012

Tim Farrell AIFD, AAF, PFCI – 2007

Janet Frye AIFD – 2011, 2012

Anne Gallagher AIFD – 2007, 2010, 2011

Lee Gallison AIFD – 2011, 2012

Darcie Garcia – 2008, 2009, 2010, 2011, 2012

Lisa Green AIFD, AAF, PFCI – 2007

Gerry Gregg AIFD – 2011, 2012

Bailey Hale – 2008

Beth Hall – 2012

Dave Hamilton – 2007-2012

Mary Hamilton – 2010

Corey Harbour AIFD, PFCI – 2008, 2009

Ruth Hendry – 2012

Deborah Holten – 2011

Andy Hopper – 2010, 2011

Melissa Huston – 2011, 2012

Armas Koehler – 2008

Adelaide Linn AIFD – 2009, 2010, 2011, 2012

Mary Lorek – 2008

Mandy Majerik AIFD, PFCI – 2011

Heidi Mae – 2007, 2008

Jacob McCall AIFD – 2011

Tony Medlock AIFD, AAF, PFCI, A_ZMF – 2011

Bill Murphy AIFD – 2011, 2012

Kimberly Nelson – 2011, 2012

Mukesh Patel AIFD – 2007

Donna Piorko AIFD – 2007, 2010, 2011, 2012

Alfred Price – 2007, 2009, 2010, 2011

Robert Quartucci – 2012

Andrew Schaffer – 2007, 2008, 2009, 2010

Amanda Schaffer – 2007, 2008, 2009, 2010

Maria Schaffer-Wright – 2007, 2008

Sandy Schroeck AIFD, PFCI – 2012

Cherrie Silverman AIFD, CPF – 2010, 2011

Paul Simpson AIFD – 2008

Ludmila Soloshenko – 2011

Timea Takacs – 2011

Carrie Thengvall – 2012

Shannon Toll – 2010, 2011, 2012

Heather Towne – 2008

Renee Tucci – 2008, 2009, 2010, 2011, 2012

Sue Weisser AIFD – 2011

Linda Wharton – 2011, 2012

Amanda Wynne – 2007, 2010

Donald Yim AIFD – 2007

ABBREVIATIONS

AAF ◆ American Academy of Floriculture

AIFD ◆ American Institute of Floral Designers

A_ZMF ◆ Arizona Master Florist

CPF ◆ Colorado Professional Florist

FBFA ◆ Fellow of the British Florist Association

NDSF ◆ National Diploma of the Society of Floristry

PFCI ◆ Professional Floral Communicators International

PARTNERS

Accent Décor Inc. | www.accentdecor.com

Amy's Orchids™ | www.amysorchids.com

Bill Kratt Photography | www.billkrattphotography.com

Bloom Japan Group™ | www.bloom-japan.net

CinemaCake Filmmakers™ | www.cinemacake.com

Delaware Valley Wholesale Florist ™ | www.dvflora.com

Design Master® | www.dmcolor.com

Eventions Productions™ | www.eventionsproductions.com

Eufloria® Flowers | www.eufloria.com

Feehly Photography | www.feehlyphotography

FloraCraft® | www.floracraft.com

Green Point Nurseries | www.greenpointnursery.com

Passion Growers™ | www.passiongrowers.com

P&F – Plantes & Flores Ornamentales™ | www.pyfosa.com

Smithers-Oasis Company™ – Oasis® Floral Products | www.oasisfloral.com

Wish Painting & Sculpture™ | www.wishpainting.com

PHOTOGRAPHERS

Bill Kratt Photography™ | www.billkrattphotography.com

Carole Sevilla Brown | www.ecosystemgardening.com

Feehly Photography™ | www.feehlyphotography.com

John Fisher

Laura Blanchard

Love Shack Photo™ | www.loveshackphoto.com

Penny Hansen Photography™ | www.pennyhansenphoto.com

Wish Painting & Sculpture™ | www.wishpainting.com